# A Dictionary of Hong Kong English

# A Dictionary of
# Hong Kong English
## Words from the Fragrant Harbor

Patrick J. Cummings and
Hans-Georg Wolf

香港大學出版社
HONG KONG UNIVERSITY PRESS

**Hong Kong University Press**
14/F Hing Wai Centre
7 Tin Wan Praya Road
Aberdeen
Hong Kong
www.hkupress.org

ISBN  978-988-8083-30-5

British Library Cataloguing-in-Publication Data
A catalogue copy for this book is available from
the British Library.

10   9   8   7   6   5   4   3   2   1

Printed and bound by Condor Production Company
Limited in Hong Kong, China

To all the speakers of English in Hong Kong
who have worked so diligently to learn
another language,
be it English, Cantonese or any other.

# Contents

# Acknowledgements

We would like to thank the following people who have contributed to the publication of this book: First of all, Patrick's wife, Carrie Cummings (Chu Ka-lai, 朱嘉麗), was our source of reference for questions related to Cantonese in general and the Chinese characters used in this dictionary. Hans-Georg's research assistant, Stefanie Reden, helped us greatly with formatting the entries and managing the files. Clara Ho from Hong Kong University Press has been an exceptionally meticulous, reliable, and efficient partner at all stages of the publication process. We also appreciate the favorable assessment and advice of the anonymous reviewers.

# Introduction

This dictionary is the first of its kind, in more than one way. Despite the fact that established and identifiable second-language varieties of English exist around the world, respective variety-specific dictionaries are still rare. As to Hong Kong English (HKE), apart from short lists of HKE words (Bolton 2002), no other compendium of HKE vocabulary has so far been written.

The exact status of HKE may still be a matter of debate among linguists and the informed public, yet what is indisputable is the unique character of HKE. This character has been shaped by Hong Kong's (colonial) history, its socio-cultural and political environment, and, most of all, the language that is predominantly spoken there, Cantonese. The entries in this dictionary, ranging from the sacred to the profane, in many ways reflect the linguistic, historical, cultural, and political situation of Hong Kong. At the same time, this reference work is a further step towards legitimizing HKE as an independent variety of English.

What is, what is not included in this dictionary? First of all, only words and word senses that are particular to HKE or have a specific reference to Hong Kong are listed. To take the example of **astronaut**, the general sense of "a person traveling or working in space," common to all varieties of English, is not considered, but only the sense specific to HKE, "a (male) person working abroad and living apart from his family." "Particular" does not mean "exclusive." In other words, although most of the words and senses in this dictionary are specific to HKE, we do not claim that none of the items can occur or be used in a similar way in another variety. If that should be the case, they are most likely to be found in other varieties of Asian English. A case in point is the HKE word **shroff**, which comes from Indian English, and is still used in Indian English and Sri Lankan English. Some items that are part of the "common core" of English, such as **crossed cheque** or **triad** have been included, because they are used far more frequently in HKE than in other varieties and this use is indicative of a socio-cultural salience. **Crossed cheque**, for example, occurs eight times in the Hong Kong component of the International Corpus of English, but is not found in the British English component. We have also included some archaic items, such as **chopped dollar** or **chop boat**, which are no longer part of common usage, but can still be found in some historical contexts.

The entries come from a variety of sources: e.g., English-language newspapers based in Hong Kong, especially the *South China Morning Post* and *The Standard*; cartoons and literary works by such authors as Larry Feign and Nury Vittachi; government information published in Hong Kong; student essays, spoken language heard on TV and in the streets every day; and internet websites from Hong Kong. Where possible, we identified the source language or variety other than Standard English, for loan words (e.g., **dim sum**) and hybrid forms (e.g., **tai-tai lunch**), but not for loan translations—which are quite frequent in HKE (e.g., **one big pot wages**). In most cases, the source is Cantonese or Mandarin (Putonghua), but there are also instances of input from others, e.g., Indian English and Malay. In cases where one particular source language cannot be clearly established, the possible source languages are indicated.

Except for some place names—where we did not see the need to document usage—and cases where the sheer number of spelling variants would have overstretched the entry, each entry, sense, and spelling variant comes with an authentic text example (in some instances slightly modified for stylistic or typographical reasons) to document usage and context. Illustrations for a number of items are also provided. We follow the convention of classifying the entries as noun (*n.*), verb (*v.*), adverb (*adv.*), adjective (*adj.*), prefix, suffix, interjection, fixed expression, and idiomatic expression. If spelling variants are too far removed from the main entry, they are listed as separate entries with a cross-reference. The most common variant is listed as main entry.

Besides a supplement of maps, this dictionary has five additional features (listed here not in the order of appearance). The first one is a list of acronyms and abbreviations commonly found in HKE. The second one is a collection of place name changes in Hong Kong and other parts of Asia, bearing evidence of the tension between a colonial past and a post-colonial presence. The third feature is a list of lexical items that have found their way from Hong Kong English to other varieties of English, i.e., are used internationally now. The fourth feature is an explication of culture-specific conceptualizations underlying some of the HKE items. The reader will notice that certain entries come with additional lexicographic information specifying what is called "conceptual domain" in linguistics, and mappings across these domains. Here, we follow a recent and innovative trend in lexicography that aims to systematize cultural information and make it explicit for speakers of other languages and varieties (Wolf and Polzenhagen 2010). The domains and respective conceptualizations, as well as their lexical instantiations, are assembled in a thesaurus-like appendix. In no other variety-dictionary has this approach been applied yet.

Although this dictionary is relatively short, we do hope readers will enjoy looking up words they have come across when visiting or living in Hong Kong, and discovering facets of Hong Kong life and culture—past and present—hitherto unknown to them.

# English in Hong Kong

## *The history of English in Hong Kong*

Hong Kong is a political, cultural and linguistic borderland. European and Chinese cultures met in 1517, when the Portuguese started trading along the south coast of China. In the seventeenth century, the English came to the area, which became a linguistic contact zone between English, Portuguese, Chinese, and other languages. When a common language was unavailable, many people communicated in Chinese Pidgin English, the newly formed trade language spoken by both Western and Asian merchants along the south coast of China in the eighteenth and nineteenth centuries. Chinese Pidgin English was a simple language that combined words from several different languages: Malay, Portuguese, Indian English, Cantonese as well as Standard English. Even today in coastal trade cities like Hong Kong and Shanghai, the local English contains relics of Chinese Pidgin English.

When the UK colonized Hong Kong after the Opium wars in 1840–43 and 1856–60, new political boundaries were created. During the UK colonial period, many Indians worked in Hong Kong, and Indian English came to have a great lexical influence on HKE (and, in turn, HKE on Indian English). Education in missionary schools, and the need for middlemen between the English and Chinese-language groups, helped develop a bilingual Eurasian comprador class. With the late twentieth-century expansion of education and growing English proficiency among the population, the comprador class became obsolete.

Following the 1997 handover of sovereignty to China, many boundaries have remained intact. Today, Hong Kong has multiple language boundaries, between different varieties of English (many of which spoken by expatriates), *Chinglish* (a mixture of Cantonese and English, whose linguistic status is still disputed; see entry for **Chinglish**), Cantonese, Putonghua and other languages such as Tagalog and Japanese.

### The status of English in Hong Kong

Cantonese is the main and most widely-spoken language of Hong Kong. It is the first language of the vast majority of Hongkongers (89.2%, according to CIA 2010). It is also a common medium of primary and secondary education. However, the importance of English in Hong Kong goes well beyond the simple role of a colonial language after the colonizers have left. In the public life of Hong Kong, so much English is used that it is possible for expatriates to live in this city for many years without ever learning Cantonese or any Chinese dialect, and many do. At the political level, the government of China recognizes the need for English in politics and law, by including English as a second official language in the Basic Law:

> In addition to the Chinese language, English may also be used as an official language by the executive authorities,

legislature and judiciary of the Hong Kong Special Administrative Region. (*The Basic Law*, Chapter I: General Principles, Article 9)

The number of speakers of English has been increasing drastically from just 6.6% in 1983 to 43% in 2001, as the latest census results indicate (Bolton 2002b: 2). The greatest increase in the popularity of English has been after the UK agreed to hand over the territory to the People's Republic of China, not during the previous century of occupation. This trend suggests a delinking of English from its colonial legacy.

English is taught in schools as a second language, along with Putonghua, and sometimes used as the medium of instruction. Most university classes are conducted in English. English is needed for people to advance in many professions, such as banking. Yet schools treat English as a foreign language. Many English teachers will not accept local words in their classrooms, and English is still taught according to a British English standard, though hardly ever attained. This strict preference for some form of British English on the side of the educators is in stark contrast to the post-colonial attraction to English mentioned above.

In Hong Kong language loyalty can be a big argument, as the debate over medium of instruction has shown. Some people express a nationalist loyalty to Putonghua. Others insist on British English being taught. Unlike what might have been expected after the 1997 handover, Putonghua has not replaced English, and English is still perceived to provide the best opportunities for success or prestige. Despite this, Putonghua, being the national language of China, will certainly be of increasing economic importance and its adoption by future generations is very likely.

## What is Hong Kong English and who are its speakers?

Closely connected to the historical phases sketched above, there have been three different types of HKE. Some overlap exists as later types have inherited some words from earlier types. Chinese Pidgin English, while not understandable to most modern English speakers, was the first type of English to develop on the south coast of China. It was used mostly by traders and businessmen. The second type of English in Hong Kong was colonial English, with influences from Indian laborers and soldiers. The third is modern HKE, which is heavily influenced by borrowing from Cantonese and is mostly, though not exclusively, used by Cantonese first-language speakers. It is this type of HKE that is represented in this dictionary.

Is HKE a Chinese language? Originally, HKE speakers were UK and Indian merchants and their employees. However, today most speakers of HKE are ethnic Hong Kong Chinese and Cantonese first-language speakers. As much as Hongkongers are Chinese, HKE, in a cultural and social sense, has become a Chinese language, although, linguistically of course, it is not part of the Sino-Tibetan language family and it includes many non-Chinese lexical features. Albeit that the majority of HKE speakers are Cantonese, HKE is spoken by speakers from a variety of ethnic backgrounds, including Old China Hands who speak English as their first language and people from other places, such as India, Pakistan, and the Philippines. This broad range of influences has shaped HKE. It has distinctly local words, but is not strictly bound geographically or even ethnically. HKE contains, inter alia, British, American, Singaporean, and Indian influences and does not exist as an isolated variety. This mélange is intrinsic to HKE and reflective of Hong Kong's past and present.

The independence of HKE has been limited by the lack of a local language authority. Reference works, such as encyclopedias, dictionaries, usage guides, and so on, are linguistic landmarks still missing for HKE. As pointed out above, many schools prefer to claim British English, of an unspecified type, as their standard and foreign teachers to teach it. That is to say, a colonal perspective will prevail as long as children are taught that "British English" is what they should aspire to. Without a recognized local standard there is little basis for a local teacher fluent in English to challenge a native speaker's opinion on how English should be used. This dictionary hopes to make a modest contribution to the recognition of HKE as a legitimate and independent variety of English.

# A Guide to Pronunciation

In cases where the pronunciation of an entry is not self-evident for a speaker of English, i.e., especially words of Cantonese or Mandarin (Putonghua) origin, we have provided a guide to the pronunciation of these words (an exception are archaic words like **yeuk**, whose pronunciation and Chinese characters could not be verified). Admittedly, it was not always easy to decide on the exact phonetic form of an entry, if an "exact" form exists at all. First of all, variation exists, for example, as regards the pronunciation of <a>. An anglicized pronunciation may tend towards /æ/ (a vowel that does not exist in Cantonese), a Cantonese towards /a(:)/ or /ʌ/. Furthermore, the vowel inventory of Cantonese is still a matter of debate, and so is the (perceived) duration of vowel length. Cantonese has a smaller vowel inventory than Standard English, and the phonetic realization of certain vowels shows allophonic variation depending on the phonetic environment (Barrie 2003). Similar problems hold true for Mandarin. In parallel, HKE is a variety whose phonology is neither fixed nor fully established (Hung 2002). To keep matters simple, we follow a broad transcription, and, on the one hand, have ignored Cantonese phonemes foreign to the L1-speaker of English, such as /y/ and /œ:/. On the other hand, we have subsumed the English monophthongs /ɪ/ and /ɒ/ under /i/ and /ɔ/ respectively. Given that Cantonese and Mandarin are tonal languages, stress markers are only provided for a small number of words that stem from other languages. The suggested pronunciations in this dictionary are thus only approximations and abstractions of actual phonetic realizations, and the phonetic forms may reflect L1-interference from different groups of speakers of HKE peculiar to this variety. The following table illustrates the phonetic symbols used in this dictionary.

## *Phonetic symbols used in the dictionary*

### Vowels and dipthongs

| Phonetic symbol (IPA) | Examples (RP) |
|---|---|
| i | lady/see/hit |
| e | bed |
| æ | flat |
| ʌ | mud |
| a(:) | father (also short vowel) |
| u(:) | cook/boot |
| ə | achieve |
| ɔ(:) | law/lot |
| ɜː | nurse |
| aɪ | pie |
| əʊ | go |
| eɪ | tray |
| ɔɪ | joy |
| aʊ | town |

## Consonants

| Phonetic symbol (IPA) | Examples (RP) |
| :---: | :---: |
| p | **p**ot |
| b | **b**ig |
| t | **t**o |
| d | **d**uck |
| k | **c**at |
| g | **g**ood |
| f | **f**irst |
| v | **v**ase |
| s | **s**it |
| z | hou**s**es |
| ʃ | **sh**oe |
| tʃ | **ch**ip |
| dƷ | **j**u**dg**e |
| h | **h**igh |
| m | **m**ilk |
| n | **n**o |
| ŋ | bri**ng** |
| w | **w**ine |
| r | **r**ed |
| l | **l**ike |
| j | **y**oung |

# References and Suggested Further Readings

Barrie, Mike. 2003. Contrast in Cantonese vowels. *Toronto Working Papers in Linguistics* 20: 1–19. Available at http://individual.utoronto.ca/michael_barrie/TWPL20.Barrie.pdf. Accessed December 16, 2010.

Bolton, Kingsley (ed.). 2002a. *Hong Kong English: Autonomy and Creativity*. Hong Kong: Hong Kong University Press.

Bolton, Kingsley. 2002b. Introduction: Hong Kong English: Autonomy and creativity. In Kingsley Bolton (ed.), *Hong Kong English: Autonomy and Creativity*, 1–25. Hong Kong: Hong Kong University Press.

Bolton, Kingsley. 2003. *Chinese Englishes*. Cambridge: Cambridge University Press.

Chan, Mimi, and Kwok, Helen. 1985. *A Study of Lexical Borrowing from Chinese into English*. Hong Kong: Hong Kong University Press.

CIA. 2010. *The World Factbook*. https://www.cia.gov/library/publications/the-world-factbook/. Accessed August 3, 2010.

Cummings, Patrick Jean. 2007. A study of lexical innovations in Hong Kong English. Unpublished M.A. dissertation, the University of Hong Kong. Available at the University of Hong Kong library.

Feign, Larry. n.d. *The World of Lily Wong*. http://www.lilywong.net/index.html. Accessed December 16, 2010.

Hung, Tony T. N. 2002. Towards a phonology of Hong Kong English. In Kingsley Bolton, (ed.), *Hong Kong English: Autonomy and Creativity*, 119–140. Hong Kong: Hong Kong University Press.

Hutton, Christopher, and Bolton, Kingsley. 2005. *A Dictionary of Cantonese Slang: The Language of Hong Kong Movies, Street Gangs and City Life*. London: C. Hurst and Co. (hardcover); Honolulu: University of Hawai'i Press (paperback).

Scott, Janet Lee. 2007. *For Gods, Ghosts and Ancestors: The Chinese Tradition of Paper Offerings*. Hong Kong: Hong Kong University Press.

Setter, Jane, Wong, Cathy S. P. and Chan, Brian H. S. 2010. *Hong Kong English*. Edinburgh University Press.

Smith, Geoff, P. and Matthews, Stephen (eds.). 2005. Chinese Pidgin English: Texts and Contexts. *Special Issue of the Hong Kong Journal of Applied Linguistics*, 10(1).

Tam, Kwok-kan, and Weiss, Timothy (eds.). 2004. *English and Globalization: Perspectives from Hong Kong and Mainland China*. Hong Kong: Chinese University Press.

Wolf, Hans-Georg and Polzenhagen, Frank. 2010. The "new semantics" of lexicography: Cognitive Sociolinguistics in L2-varieties of English. *LAUD Linguistic Agency*. Series A: General and Theoretical Papers, No. 766.

# A Guide to Frequency

We decided to give the readers an idea of the frequency of the items listed in HKE usage. Our data is based on brief Google.hk surveys using the Hong Kong region restriction at different times in the year 2010. Admittedly, this specification does not allow for a high degree of accuracy, and there are limits to the reliability of this approach. First, Google.hk may also list sites unrelated to Hong Kong. Second, our analysis only gives a snaphot of frequency of usage at a certain period of time on the internet, which may lead to the overrepresentation of an item because it has a certain salience due to its being a "hot issue" in the media (a case in point is **compensated dating**). Third, some entries we labeled "archaic" may still be frequently found in written sources with historical reference but hardly in contemporary discourse (e.g., **Celestial Empire/Kingdom**). Nevertheless, the readers may still find this feature useful to fathom the importance or widespreadedness of the items included in this dictionary. For the different variant forms and senses of an entry, the frequency is combined. The key to the frequency symbols is a follows:

★★★★★ : obscure and/or archaic

★★★★★ : less than 20 occurrences on Google.hk

★★★★★ : from 20 to 150 occurrences on Google.hk

★★★☆☆ : less than 1,000 occurrences on Google.hk

★★★★☆ : less than 10,000 occurrences on Google.hk

★★★★★ : more than 10,000 occurrences on Google.hk

? : No assessment possible because of competing forms (e.g., names of persons)

# Common Acronyms and Abbreviations

Hong Kong English has many acronyms. The colloquial ones or the ones that phonetically have become a word of their own occur as separate entries in the dictionary. The others are included in the following list.

**Note:** In the case of some government agencies, their names are changed too often to make recording them worthwhile, e.g., EB/EDB (Education Bureau), ED (Education Department), EMB (Education and Manpower Bureau).

| | |
|---|---|
| ADPL | Association for Democracy and People's Livelihood (a pro-democracy political group) |
| ASEAN | Association of South East Asian Nations |
| ATV | Asia Television |
| BCA | Basic Competency Assessments (tests of students' progress) |
| CCP | Chinese Communist Party |
| CCTV | China Central Television |
| CE | Chief Executive (of the Hong Kong Special Administrative Region of the People's Republic of China) |

| | |
|---|---|
| CID | Central Intelligence Division of the Hong Kong Police Force |
| CityU | City University of Hong Kong |
| CLP | The China Light and Power Company |
| CMB | China Motor Bus (CMB was the first franchised bus company in Hong Kong; it lost the franchise in 1998.) |
| CPH | Castle Peak Hospital |
| CR | The Companies Registry |
| CSSA | The Comprehensive Social Security Assistance Scheme |
| CUHK | The Chinese University of Hong Kong |
| DAB | The Democratic Alliance for the Betterment and Progress of Hong Kong (a pro-Beijing political group) |
| DSS | The Direct Subsidy Scheme (government funding for schools) |
| EIA | Environmental Impact Assessment |
| ESD | The Electronic Service Delivery Scheme (government) |
| ESF | The English Schools Foundation |
| ExCo | The Executive Council (advisors to the Chief Executive) |
| FDW | Foreign domestic workers |
| FTU | The Federation of Trade Unions |
| HA | Hospital Authority, Housing Authority |

# Common Acronyms and Abbreviations

| | |
|---|---|
| HK | Hong Kong |
| HKALE | The Hong Kong Advanced Level Examination* |
| HKAPA | The Hong Kong Academy for Performing Arts |
| HKBH | Hong Kong Buddhist Hospital |
| HKBU | Hong Kong Baptist University |
| HKCAAVQ | Hong Kong Council for Accreditation of Academic and Vocational Qualifications |
| HKCEE | The Hong Kong Certificate of Education Examination* |
| HKCTU | The Hong Kong Confederation of Trade Unions (a pro-democracy organization) |
| HKDSE | The Hong Kong Diploma of Secondary Education Examination* |
| HKEAA | The Hong Kong Examinations and Assessment Authority |
| HKer | Hong Kong person |
| HKEx | Hong Kong Exchanges and Clearing Limited |
| HKFE | Hong Kong Futures Exchange |
| HKIEd | The Hong Kong Institute of Education |

---

\* The HKCEE and the HKALE will be phased out and replaced by the Hong Kong Diploma of Secondary Education Examination (HKDSE).

# Common Acronyms and Abbreviations

| | |
|---|---|
| HKMA | The Hong Kong Monetary Authority |
| HKSAR | The Hong Kong Special Administrative Region of the People's Republic of China |
| HKSYU | Hong Kong Shue Yan University |
| HKU | The University of Hong Kong |
| HKUST | The Hong Kong University of Science and Technology |
| HOS | The Home Ownership Scheme |
| HSBC | The HongKong and Shanghai Banking Corporation |
| HIS | The Hang Seng Index |
| ICAC | The Independent Commission Against Corruption |
| IPO | Initial Public Offering |
| JUPAS | The Joint University Programmes Admissions System |
| KCR | The Kowloon–Canton Railroad |
| KCRC | The Kowloon–Canton Railroad Corporation |
| KMB | The Kowloon Motor Bus Company |
| KMT | The Kuomintang of China |
| KWH | Kwong Wah Hospital |
| LegCo | The Legislative Council |
| LRT | The Light Rail Transit |
| LSD | The League of Social Democrats |
| LU | Lingnan University |

| | |
|---|---|
| MMRC | MacLehose Medical Rehabilitation Centre |
| MPF | Mandatory Provident Fund Scheme (public pension plan) |
| MTR | Mass Transit Railway |
| MTRC | Mass Transit Railway Corporation |
| NDH | North District Hospital |
| NET | Native English Teacher |
| NT | The New Territories |
| OCTB | Organised Crime and Triad Bureau of the Hong Kong Police Force |
| OLMH | Our Lady of Maryknoll Hospital |
| OMELCO | Office of the Members of the Executive and Legislative Councils of Hong Kong |
| OUHK | The Open University of Hong Kong |
| PCCW | The Pacific Century Cyberworks (telecommunications provider in HK) |
| PLA | The People's Liberation Army |
| PMH | Princess Margaret Hospital |
| PolyU | The Hong Kong Polytechnic University |
| PRC | The People's Republic of China |
| PTU | The Professional Teacher's Union or the Police Tactical Unit of the Hong Kong Police Force |
| PWH | Prince of Wales Hospital |
| PYNEH | Pamela Youde Nethersole Eastern Hospital |

| | |
|---|---|
| QEH | Queen Elizabeth Hospital |
| QGO | The Queensway Government Offices |
| QMH | Queen Mary Hospital |
| RGC | The Research Grants Council |
| RTHK | Radio Television Hong Kong, formerly Royal Television Hong Kong |
| SAR | Special Administrative Region |
| SCMP | The South China Morning Post |
| SEHK | The Stock Exchange of Hong Kong Limited |
| SEZ | Special Economic Zone |
| SSPA | The Secondary School Places Allocation (System) |
| TCM | Traditional Chinese Medicine |
| TKOH | Tseung Kwan O Hospital |
| TMH | Tuen Mun Hospital |
| TSA | The Territory-wide System Assessment (part of the BCA) |
| TST | Tsim Sha Tsui |
| TVB | Television Broadcasts Limited |
| TWGH | Tung Wah Group of Hospitals |
| UGC | The University Grants Committee |
| VTC | The Vocational Training Council |
| YCH | Yan Chai Hospital |

# A

# ABC

*idiomatic expression.*

**Definition:** ❶ American-born Chinese; ❷ Australian-born Chinese.

**Text example:**

"We have several kinds of Chinese alone: Hong Kong Chinese, Mainland Chinese, Taipei Chinese, and not to mention the other overseas Chinese such as the **ABC** (American- or Australian-born Chinese) or the BBC (British-born Chinese)."

# acting-up

*fixed expression.*

**Definition:** acting at a grade higher than one's current grade or rank (e.g., in the Civil Service).

**Text example:**

"In the case of **acting-up** with replacement (this involves acting in a functional post which carries a higher maximum salary point than that of the teacher's substantive rank) ... the rate will be revised to 100% after the first 180 calendar days of acting."

See: **doubling-up**.

# ah-ba

/əh ba:/ *n.*

**Source language:** Cantonese (阿爸).

**Definition:** father (affectionate and informal).

**Text example:**

"Through Jesus, who is our Brother, we both have God as our Father, whom we are encouraged to address in the most intimate and childlike way as 'Abba' (how close to the Chinese '**Ah Ba**'; also to the Indians 'Appa'!) and we have Mary as our Mother."

# ah-cha

/əh tʃaː/ *n.*
**Source language:** Cantonese (阿叉).
**Definition:** a derogatory term for people from the Indian sub-continent, including Nepalis and Pakistanis.
**Text example:**

"The crew members called Mitra '**Ah Cha**', the derogatory term for South Asians living in Hong Kong, many of whom were seen as associated with jobs like security guards, according to Tang's recollection of those common prejudices."

# aided school

*n.*
**Definition:** a school that receives subsidies from the government.
**Text example:**

"The site for an **aided school** is granted to the sponsor by private treaty at a nominal premium, except where it lies within a Housing Authority estate, in which case the school operates under a tenancy agreement between the sponsor and the authority."

# aiyeeah (also ayah)

/aɪːjaː/ *interjection.*
**Source language:** Cantonese (哎吔).
**Definition:** a common verbal exclamation, used as an emphatic marker expressing surprise or the feeling that some news is perceived as a burden or imposition.
**Text example:**

❶ "**Aiyeeah**! I did not lie to her."
❷ "We'd have these meetings and you say you wanted to put a road through here or cut away a bit of the hill

there; they'd suck in their breath and announce, '**Ayah**, very difficult, that's the dragon's head.' "

**Note:** The spelling varies greatly.

# alphabets

*n.*

**Definition:** letters of the alphabet.

**Text example:**

"Ms Lau said that the President of the Lingnan University had reportedly said that some 95% of the university's first-year students could not accurately pronounce the 26 **alphabets** of English."

# amah

/'aːmaː/ *n.*

**Source variety:** Indian English.

**Definition:** a female domestic servant.

**Text example:**

"Whether they are called domestic servants, housekeepers, governesses, nurse-maids, household helpers, domestic helpers, maids or **amahs**, the 165,000 Filipinas (1996 figure) have made it possible for the expatriate wife to enjoy activities outside her home."

See: **ayah**, **ya-ya**.

**Note:** Also used in compounds, such as *cook amah, wash amah, general amah, baby amah, coolie amah*, etc.

# ancient egg

*n.*

See: **century egg**.

# A quality

*adj., n.*

**Definition:** the higher grade of (counterfeit) products.

**Text example:**

"Take for example the building of a prison. If it has been agreed that **A quality** bricks will be used, and the civil servant checking the matter agrees to B quality, the contractor will save enormous amounts of money, and the civil servant should be rewarded accordingly."

**Spoken example:**

"'How much is this Gucci handbag?' '400, it's **A quality**, made in Taiwan.'"

See: **B quality**.

# A share

*fixed expression.*

**Definition:** corporate shares on the Shanghai and Shenzhen stock exchanges that are traded in Renminbi for purchase by PRC citizens only.

**Text example:**

"The real distinction between an **'A' share** and a red chip is very blurred. People use the two terms intermixed very often."

See: **B shares**, **red chip**.

# astronaut

*idiomatic expression.*

**Definition:** a (male) person working abroad and living apart from his family.

**Text example:**

"The epithet '**astronaut**,' used before 1997 to describe Chinese seekers of foreign passports who spent a great deal of time flying to visit wives and children sent on ahead to establish residence in North America or Australia, has been dusted down and reapplied, this time to expatriates."

# auntie (also aunty)

*n.*

**Definition:** ❶ a friendly form of address for female persons above one's age; ❷ a female friend of a person's parents who is not a biological relation.

**Text example:**

❶ "Lily Marie Kwok (we call her **Auntie** Marie), a thirty-something Thai-Chinese woman and the shopkeeper of Good-luck shoe shop, has great zeal in mahjong playing."

❷ "Don't you remember when we were little ... that trick Mum played on **Aunty** Winnie ... she dressed you up as me and when **Aunty** Winnie came round she thought you WERE me."

**Underlying conceptualizations:** A MEMBER OF SOCIETY IS A MEMBER OF THE FAMILY, A FRIEND OF THE PARENTS IS A MEMBER OF THE FAMILY [TARGET DOMAINS ➡ MEMBER OF SOCIETY, PARENTAL FRIEND] [SOURCE DOMAIN ➡ FAMILY].

See: **uncle**.

# auntie (visiting, coming)

*idiomatic expression.*

**Definition:** menstrual period.

**Text example:**

"They have been going out together for a number of years and have been trying to save up a little nest egg to enter into married life with—but events are put on fast forward when Maggie announces that '**Auntie has not come** for a long while.'"

**Note:** This term tends to be used in oral communication between females only.

visiting , coming

# ayah

/aɪːjaː/ *n.*

**Source language:** Portuguese.

**Definition:** a female domestic servant.

**Text example:**

"Many of us brought up in Asia owe a great debt to our nannies. She was our amah, **ayah** and yaya."

See: **amah**, **ya-ya**.

# B

bai san
bak choi
bamboo snake
banana
ban mui
bashi hou
BBC
Beida
big brother
big sister
bird's nest
black fungus
boat congee
BoHo
boiled egg
bok choy
bone girl
bor law yau
Boundary Street
B quality
B shares
bubble tea
Buddha's Birthday

# bai san

/baɪ saːn/ *adj., n.*

**Source language:** Cantonese (拜山).

**Definition:** a style of prayer.

**Text example:**

❶ "One of the drivers detoured to a mini-shrine. He extracted three joss sticks, applied the lighter, and bowed twice in solemn **bai san** fashion, which is when you bow to the shrine with joss sticks in your hands."

❷ "In recognition of Chinese tradition, a fung shui expert gave advice on the removal of the School's centre flag pole, after which a **bai-san** ceremony was held to bless, bring good fortune and luck to the grounds." ★★★★☆

**bai san** (drawing by Adrian Cennydd Petyt)

# bak choi

/bək tʃɔɪ/ *n.*

See: **bok choy**. ★★★☆☆

# bamboo snake

*n.*

**Definition:** *Trimeresurus albolabris*, elsewhere known as "green pit viper," the most common venomous snake found in HK.

**Text example:**

"**Bamboo Snake** (venomous) Description: A medium-sized snake, averaging 50 cm in total length, but can reach up to 90 cm."

# banana

*idiomatic expression.*

**Definition:** a Westernized Chinese person (derogatory).

**Text example:**

"The use of bamboo also has the connotation of being Chinese. This is similar to the analogy of a **banana**, which is yellow outside but the inside is white, which is used to describe Chinese people who are born in the 'West' and therefore 'whitened.'"

# ban mui

/ba:n mɔɪ/ *n.*

**Source language:** Cantonese (賓妹).

**Definition:** a Filipina (derogatory).

**Text example:**

"The sexual representations of the Filipinas as either 'saints' or 'prostitutes' hark back to the traditional depictions of women as two-dimensional objects and currently reflect the ascribed collective identity of the FDWs (foreign domestic workers) by the Hong Kong Chinese community as '**ban mui**.'"

# bashi hou

/baːʃiː haʊ/ *n.*

**Source language:** Mandarin (八十後).

**Definition:** Hong Kong people born after 1980, especially with reference to political protests.

**Text Example:**

"**Bashi hou** Generation" (those born after 1980) became the latest local media buzzword this week. This generation is described as a bunch of angry kids who are unhappy about everything and see no future."

# BBC

*idiomatic expression.*

**Definition:** British-born Chinese.

See: **ABC**.

# Beida

/beɪ daː/ *n.*

**Definition:** Peking University.

**Source:** Mandarin (北大).

**Text example:**

"A survey in Peking University (Beida) showed that 75.4% of students in **Beida** already had or wanted to have part-time jobs; 54.5% already had or wanted to have started their own businesses."

# big brother

*fixed expression.*

**Definition:** ❶ a senior male in a triad; ❷ a male schoolmate from a senior grade or an older alumnus.

**Text example:**

❶ "On the first day after school I already followed the two classmates who put their hands on my shoulder and went to their 'territory' to see their '**Big Brother**'. I contributed a specified amount of money ... to the triad and became a 'triad member' all of a sudden."

**❷** "Peer Support Activities like co-operative learning and **big-brother**-big-sister schemes are organized to facilitate learning and social integration of students."

**Underlying conceptualization (generic):** A FELLOW MEMBER OF A SOCIAL GROUP ONE BELONGS TO IS A SIBLING [TARGET DOMAIN ➡ FELLOW MEMBER OF A SOCIAL GROUP] [SOURCE DOMAIN ➡ FAMILY].

See: **big sister**.

# big sister

*fixed expression.*

**Definition:** a female schoolmate from a senior grade or an older alumna.

See: **big brother**.

# bird's nest

*fixed expression.*

**Definition:** the edible nest of a variety of swallow; Chinese health food.

**Text example:**

"Edible **bird's nest** is one of the widely used health foods in Chinese communities."

See: **swallow nest**.

# black fungus

*n.*

**Definition:** an ear-shaped fungus, *Auricularia polytricha*, used in HK cooking.

**Text example:**

"Woo recommends cauliflower, sweet pepper and dried **black fungus**, or wan yee, which contain lots of dietary fibers that are good for those who need to be fastidious about controlling their weight and blood glucose levels."

# boat congee

*n.*

**Definition:** a popular Hong Kong variety of congee with a variety of ingredients, often including seafood, pork and tofu.

**Text example:**

"Nutrient Contents of Indigenous Congee, Rice and Noodle Dishes: **Boat congee**."

See: **sampan congee, congee**.

# BoHo

*n.*

**Definition:** "below Hollywood Road," an area of HK Island.

**Text example:**

"While most of Hong Kong lives in noise and loves it, there is always a gang of grouchy malcontents who prize a bit of quiet. When SoHo doesn't give them a sufficiency, they betake themselves to **BoHo**."

# boiled egg

*idiomatic expression.*

**Definition:** a Chinesized Western person (derogatory), with reference to skin color.

**Text example:**

"**boiled egg**, white on the outside, yellow on the inside."

# bok choy (also bak choi, pak choi, pak choy)

/bək tʃɔɪ/ /pək tʃɔɪ/ *n.*

**Source language:** Cantonese (白菜).

**Definition:** a popular kind of cabbage, of the species *Brassica rapa* var. *chinensis*.

**Text example:**

❶ "There are also rich choices of vegetables, e.g. choy sum, spinach, **bok choy**, wax gourd, hairy gourd, dried mushroom and straw mushroom, etc."

❷ "Most good Hong Kong restaurants serve many all-vegetarian dishes, large varieties of choi sum, **bak choi**, Chinese spinach, broccoli, beans, taro, and other succulent dishes."

❸ "Boil **pak choi** until tender and dice finely."

❹ "Shanghainese noodles, sui kwa (with pork and **pak choy**), pure soymilk."

**bok choy** (drawing by Adrian Cennydd Petyt)

# bone girl

*idiomatic expression.*

**Definition:** a woman who provides massage but also sex services.

**Text example:**

"**Bone Girl** (BG) normally not provide outdoor service, or at a very very expensive price, so it's not suggest to do so."

# bor law yau

/bɔ lɔ jau/ *n.*

**Source language:** Cantonese (菠蘿油).

**Definition:** a sweet bun served or stuffed with butter.

**Text example:**

> "Our next generation may never be able to savour the working man's delight of **bor law yau**, the caramel-led bun served with a thick slab of butter."

# Boundary Street

*n.*

**Definition:** a street that historically marked the boundary between the southern part of Kowloon, taken from China in 1860, and New Kowloon, which remained part of China until it was leased as part of the New Territories in 1898 for 99 years.

See: **New Kowloon, New Territories**.

# B quality

*adj., n.*

**Definition:** the lower grade of (counterfeit) products.

**Text example:** see **A quality**.

**Spoken example:**

> "No B quality, is **A quality**."

# B shares

*n.*

**Definition:** shares traded on the Shanghai and Shenzhen stock exchanges which are traded in foreign currencies.

**Text example:**

> "On average, A-share prices were worth about one and a half times their **B-share** counterpart."

See: **A share**.

# bubble tea

*n.*

**Definition:** a sweetly-flavored tea beverage originally from Taiwan, containing tapioca balls.

**Text example:**

> "Saint's Alp's unique concoctions of East-West 'tea-shakes' have proven to be a hit among Hong Kong's teenagers. Its very popular '**bubble tea**' combines conventional teas with cocktail-like quencher recipes."

See: **pearl milk tea**.

# Buddha's Birthday

*n.*

**Definition:** statutory holiday on the eighth day of the fourth month of the Chinese lunar calendar.

**Text example:**

> "Lord **Buddha's birthday** on the 8th day of the 4th Chinese lunar month is the most important festive occasion in the life of the nunnery."

# C

# cagehome

*fixed expression.*

**Definition:** a home about 1 x 1 x 2 m in size, made from bars and used by the very poor.

**Text example:**

"Hong Kong the metropolis sees its 15,000 families taking bed-wide '**cages**' as **home** but does not have much help to offer."

⭐⭐⭐☆☆

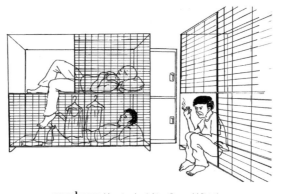

**cagehome** (drawing by Adrian Cennydd Petyt)

# cageman

*n.*

**Definition:** a man, or people who live in a cage home.

**Text example:**

"**Cageman** might have been better titled Cagepeople, because it is all about the occupants of a men's hostel in Hong Kong, who do indeed live in cages—not all the time, of course, but they sleep and keep their belongings inside them."

**Note:** The fact that no primary source could be found for *cagewoman* or *cagechild* does not mean that women and children are less likely to live in a *cagehome*. Instead, women and children are referred to indirectly as in "a child in a *cagehome*" or a women's *cagehome*.

# cagepeople

*n.*

See: **cageman**.

# candareen

/kəndə'rin/ *n.*
**Source language:** Malay.
**Definition:** 1/1600 catty or 1 fan.
**Text example:**

> "Eleven men smoking one **candareen** of opium; not a particle of craving. (It is supposed that the craving each man has for the drug is so small that he is satisfied with one-eleventh of a **candareen**, i.e., none at all.)."

See: **catty**.

# Canto

/'kæntəʊ/ *prefix.*
**Definition:** a prefix that indicates a Cantonese variety of something.

See: **Canto-pop**.

# Cantonese

*adj., n.*
**Definition:** ❶ relating to the Cantonese people, language or culture; ❷ the primary language and ethnic group in Hong Kong.
**Text example:**

❶ "**Cantonese** recipes."

❷ "In Hong Kong this has been especially true since the

1970s, and the slowly increasing use of spoken **Cantonese** and written Chinese in so-called 'high' domains such as law and government."

# Canto-pop

*n.*

**Definition:** Cantonese pop songs.

**Text example:**

"The songs are sung in Cantonese and are collectively known as '**canto-pop**.'"

# caput school

/ˈkæpət skuːl/ *n.*

**Source languages:** Latin, English.

**Definition:** a school that receives a government grant per student.

**Text example:**

"Nevertheless, the enthusiasm and dedication of teachers deeply impressed parents and the Education Department. In 1978, it was asked to become a **caput school** and before long, it was further invited to become an aided school."

**Note:** *Caput* is derived from the Latin "*per caput*," the singular of *per capita*.

# carabao

/kærəˈbaʊ/ *n.*

**Source language:** Malay.

**Definition:** water buffalo, *Bubalus bubalis carabanesis*.

**Text example:**

"But lack of capacity may hinder any possible attempt by the small dairy company to export its ice cream, which is made from the milk of the **carabao**, or water buffalo."

# Castle Peak

*n.*

**Definition:** a 583-m rocky hill next to the town of Tuen Mun. A coal-burning power station is located nearby and the area was used as a firing range by the British military.

# category I, IIA, IIB, III

*n.*

**Definition:** a rating system for film censorship.

**Text example:**

"**Category I**—represented with a circle—suitable for all ages

**Category IIA**—represented with a square—not suitable for children

**Category IIB**—represented with a square—not suitable for young persons and children

**Category III**—represented with a triangle—for persons aged 18 or above only."

# catty

/kæti:/ *n.*

**Source language:** Malay.

**Definition:** a measurement of weight, officially equal to 0.60478982 kilogram.

**Text example:**

"1 picul (tam) = 100 **catties**

1 **catty** (kan) = 0.60478982 kilogram

1 tael (leung) = 1/16 **catty**

1 mace (tsin) = 1/160 **catty**

1 candareen (fan) = 1/1600 **catty**

1 tael troy = 37.429 grams

1 mace troy = 1/10 tael troy

1 candareen troy = 1/10 mace troy."

**Note:** The weight measurements *catty*, along with *tael*, were originally borrowed from Malay. The Standard English word "tea caddy" originates from "a catty of tea," although the size of a tea caddy appears to have shrunk.

# CBC

*idiomatic expression.*
**Definition:** Canadian-born Chinese.
**Text example:**

"i speak cantonese all day ... but i always msn with the **CBC** (canadian born chinese) they don't read cantonese, so i have to use english ... i think this is the best way for me to learn english ..."

See: **ABC**, **BBC**.

# celestial

*n.*
**Definition:** a Chinese person (archaic).
**Text example:**

"Now, in the present instance, one **Celestial**, perhaps more timid than the rest, told the officer quietly and mysteriously that the 'Josses' sent the storm because some of the Chinamen had smuggled some corpses on board without paying freight for them."

**Note:** Today, this term (as an adjective) is commonly used for HK companies: *Celestial Asia Securities Holdings Ltd.*, *Celestial Assets Ltd.*, *Celestial Court*, *Celestial Digital Entertainment Ltd.*, *Celestial Healthcare*, *Celestial Pictures Ltd.*

# Celestial Empire/Kingdom

*fixed expression.*
**Definition:** the country of China (archaic).
**Text example:**

"Proud and self-contained China shunned outside contacts. In their self-proclaimed superiority, the Chinese in the 18th century still believed that only barbarians lived beyond their boundaries and that their countries were automatically vassal states of the **Celestial Kingdom**."

See: **celestial**.

# Central

*n.*

**Definition:** synonym for downtown Hong Kong or the city of Victoria.

**Text example:**

"Strict crowd control measures will be implemented by police in **Central** in anticipation of a large congregation of rowdy revelers over the festive season."

**Note:** The city is officially called Victoria, but this designation is rarely used in favor of "Central."

A bird's-eye view of **Central** and Sheung Wan,
Hong Kong, c. 1940
(Source: Public domain, Wikipedia Commons)

# Central and Western District

*n.*

**Definition:** a district in the northwestern part of Hong Kong Island, the central business district.

# century egg

*fixed expression.*

**Definition:** a preserved egg, in Chinese style.

**Text example:**

❶ "The **century egg**, also known as preserved egg, hundred-year egg, thousand-year egg, thousand-year-old egg, is a Chinese food made by preserving duck, chicken or quail eggs in a mixture of clay, ash, salt, lime, and rice straw for several weeks to several months, depending on the method of processing."

❷ "Also called **century egg**, ancient egg, Ming Dynasty egg, its proper name is pei daan (preserved egg)." ★★☆☆☆

# char chaan teng (also cha chaan teng, cha chaan tang)

/tʃa: tʃa:n təŋ/ *n.*

**Source language:** Cantonese (茶餐廳).

**Definition:** a tea and lunch shop.

**Text example:**

❶ "The **char chaan teng** is now to be found in Britain, Canada, the United States and many European countries. But in the city of its birth its demise is being hastened by the relentless march of the bulldozers ... The **cha chaan teng** is the essence of Hong Kong culture."

❷ "Make no mistake, '**cha chaan tangs**'—literally translated as tea restaurants—are not where you go 'yum cha' and eat 'dim sum.'" ★★★★☆

# char siu, also char siew, cha siu, char su (and char siu bau, char su bau, cha siu bau, char siew bau)

/tʃa: sju:/ /tʃa: sju: baʊ/ *n.*
**Source language:** Cantonese (叉燒/包).
**Definition:** roast pork, in a Hong Kong style (also roast pork bun).
**Text example:**

❶ "Chinese barbecued pork (**Char Siu**) is Cantonese-style barbecued pork ... **Char siu** is rarely eaten on its own, but used in the preparation of other foods, most notably **char siu bau**, where it is stuffed in buns, and **char siew** rice (or barbecued pork with rice)."

❷ "**Cha Siu Bao**—roast pork buns ... yum, yum!"

**char siu bau** (photo by P. J. Cummings)

# chau

/tʃaʊ/ *n.*
**Source language:** Cantonese (洲).
**Definition:** an island.
**Text example:**

"Ap Lei **Chau**," "Cheung **Chau**," "Peng **Chau**," etc.

**Note:** Usually used only in place names.

# chee-saw

/tʃiː sɔː/ *n.*
**Source language:** Cantonese (廁所).
**Definition:** toilet.
**Text example:**

"… and I tell to him that I am looking for **chee-saw**, toilet."

**Note:** Usually spoken language.

# chek

/tʃek/ *n.*
**Source language:** Cantonese (尺).
**Definition:** 0.371475 meters.
**Text example:**

"1 kilometre km = 1000 metres = 0.621371 mile = 2691.97 **cheks**

1 metre m = 3.28084 feet = 2.69197 **cheks**

1 centimetre cm = 0.01 metre = 0.393701 inch = 2.69197 fans

1 millimetre mm = 0.001 metre = 0.0393701 inch = 0.269197 fan."

# Chek Lap Kok (Airport)

/tʃek lap kɔk/ *n.*
**Source language:** Cantonese (赤鱲角).
**Definition:** an island and the new airport to the west of Victoria Harbour. Two islands were merged by reclamation to create land for the airport.

# cheong fun

/tʃʌŋ fʌn/ *n.*
**Source language:** Cantonese (腸粉).
**Definition:** a type of dim sum based on a flat, rice noodle roll.
**Text example:**

"Premium **Cheong Fun**—Shrimp (from food wrapper)."

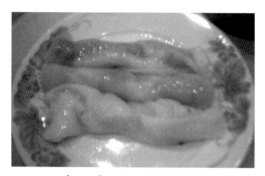

**cheong fun** (photo by P. J. Cummings)

# cheongsam

/tʃʌŋ sʌm/ *n.*

**Source language:** Cantonese (長衫).

**Definition:** a traditional Chinese dress.

**Text example:**

"A pretty girl reading a book, wearing a **cheongsam** or looking at a notebook computer in her lap would hardly pass for challenging camera-work."

**Note:** Once very formal, it is now found most often as a waitress's uniform, school uniform and when a woman is dressing in a traditional manner for a special event.

**cheongsam** (drawing by Adrian Cennydd Petyt)

# Cheung Chau Bun Festival

/tʃʌŋ tʃaʊ bʌn festivəl/ *n.*

**Source languages:** Cantonese (包山節), English. Also known as Cheung Chau Da Jiu Festival (長洲太平清醮).

**Definition:** a non-statutory holiday recently fixed to be held in Cheung Chau in the fourth month (8th day), to thank the God Pak Tai, among other activities. The buns are intended to appease the hungry ghosts of pirate victims that are said to roam the island in search of food.

**Text example:**

"After the parade is the competition that gives the celebration its slightly misleading English name of 'the **Bun Festival**'. Three towers of buns ... containing thousands of buns on each are erected next to the Bak Dai Temple and young people scramble up to the top in a frenzied bid."

See: **ghost**.

# chick, chicken

*idiomatic expression.*

**Definition:** female prostitute.

**Text example:**

"Women prostitutes are called '**chickens**' in Hong Kong, and the men are called 'ducks."

See: **duck**.

# chicken-worm

*idiomatic expression.*

**Definition:** a man who frequents prostitutes.

**Text example:**

"Hong sends **Chicken Worm** to harass Damon who in turn flushes **Chicken Worm** out from a brothel and severely punishes him."

# China doll

*idiomatic expression.*

**Definition:** a pretty young Chinese woman or girl.

**Text example:**

"The Hollywood star with the **China doll** face is as charmingly attractive as she is clever."

# Chinese

*n.*

**Definition:** Cantonese language and not Mandarin/Putonghua.

**Text example:**

"The Supplementary Language Subjects offer students opportunities for improving their English, **Chinese**, Putonghua and learning foreign languages."

# Chinese parsley

*n.*

**Definition:** coriander, a plant of the species *Coriandrum sativum*.

**Text example:**

"The wet market on Graham Street has it. But I don't think it is much cheaper than the supermarkets. My suggestion— substitute with coriander leaves (or what is also called **Chinese parsley**)."

# Chinese Valentine's Day

*n.*

**Definition:** two different non-statutory holidays; the fifteenth day of the New Year and the seventh day of the seventh lunar month.

**Text example:**

"There are many versions of the origins of **Chinese**

**Valentine's Day**. One legend involves the Goddess of Heaven and her seven daughters." ★★★★☆

# Chinglish

/tʃɪŋglɪʃ/ *n.*

**Definition:** Chinese-English code-mixing.

**Text example:**

"A huge number of overseas-educated Hong Kong Chinese have completely lost the ability to speak pure Cantonese, and communicate with each other in **Chinglish** without even realising it. Even government officials are often heard inserting English words into their sentences, in a form of **Chinglish** Lite." ★★★★☆

# Ching Ming

/tʃɪŋ mɪŋ/ *n.*

**Source language:** Cantonese (清明).

**Definition:** statutory holiday for the purpose of cleaning the tombs of ancestors, often on hillsides.

**Text example:**

"Oh how I hate these holidays. **Ching Ming** (grave sweeping festival) is supposed to be tomorrow, so why does every grave sweeper in Hong Kong come over here (Lantau Island, a famous grave place) today?" ★★★★☆

# Chippies (also Chuppies)

/tʃipiːs/ /tʃʌpiːs/ *idiomatic expression.*

**Definition:** Chinese Yuppies.

**Text example:**

❶ "Be advised, this is no beggar's holiday. Come here with full pocket and purse. And pose for the TV crews that come here to shoot scenes of well dressed people on the rise: yuppies and their Chinese counterparts, **chippies**."

❷ "How rich are these urban **Chuppies**?" ★★☆☆☆

# chit

/tʃit/ *n.*

**Source language:** Indian English.

**Definition:** a bill or similar official small piece of paper.

**Text example:**

"A truck driver hands a **chit** to the weigh bridge operator at a landfill site."
★★★★★

# chit-fund

*n.*

**Definition:** a fund to which the participants subscribe and a bidder collects the whole fund; a money-lending scheme.

**Text example:**

"Participation in a **chit-fund** is not regarded as lending money at interest nor is it regarded as borrowing from an unauthorised source."
★★★★☆

# choi sum (also **choy sum**)

/tʃɔɪ sʌm/ *n.*

**Source language:** Cantonese (菜心).

**Definition:** a popular kind of cabbage of the species *Brassica rapa* var. *parachinensis*.

**Text example:**

❶ "He was convinced there had to be more to life than growing **choi sum** and raising pigs for slaughter."

❷ "The Health Department has destroyed 3.2 tonnes of contaminated cabbage and **choy sum**, and has stepped up market surveillance." ★★★★☆

**choi sum** (drawing by Adrian Cennydd Petyt)

# chop

/tʃɔp/ *n.*

**Source languages:** Chinese Pidgin English, Indian English.

**Definition:** ❶ a seal or impression, stamp or brand; ❷ trademark, a rank of quality; ❸ a permit or official document of some kind made legally binding by the addition of such a chop.

**Text example:**

❶ "All forms must be checked and signed by either the employer/authorized officer with the Company **Chop** (if any) and/or the member (if applicable)."

❷ " 'TWIN BATS', the registered trade-mark of The World Trading & Grinding Mill, is used for all kinds of powders produced, and this '**chop**' is now well known."

❸ "The arrangement which Howqua proposes ... is that the Commodore shall permit Americans and neutrals to trade at Whampoa in consideration of which the Mandarins will connive at a smuggling trade being carried on with the British outside. But no **chop** is to be issued to this effect."

**Note:** The practice of using *chops* is common in modern HK business. The word *chop* in Chinese Pidgin English had been carried by European merchants from India to China, where it came to be used in senses that have since become archaic in India. ★★★★★

# chop-boat

*n.*

**Source language:** Indian English.

**Definition:** a merchant's boat in Hong Kong, carrying a chop note, hence having permission to trade (archaic).

**Text example:**

"It is now decided that we are to leave Canton on Tuesday or Wednesday next. They grant us a **chop-boat** to go down in."

See: **chop**.

# chop-chop

*adv.*

**Source language:** Chinese Pidgin English.

**Definition:** hurry up (mostly archaic).

**Text example:**

"Waiter! Bringee sugar for my tea, **chop chop**!"

**Note:** The use of this term today is possibly embarrassing or patronizing.

# chop-house

*n.*

**Source language:** Chinese Pidgin English.

**Definition:** a customs office, where a chop is obtained giving permission to trade (archaic).

**Text example:**

"Before returning to the steamer, the boats pulled across to the opposite side of the river, where a large **chop-house** and military depot were likewise destroyed."

# chopped dollar

*fixed expression.*

**Definition:** a dollar chopped, or stamped with a private mark, as a guarantee of its genuineness (archaic).

**Text example:**

"The bank punches its own brand on all the good dollars: this punching process, besides stamping some Chinese words on the silver, from the force of the blow makes the dollar into a little bowl. These '**chopped**' dollars ... with a handle fixed to them make unique spoons."

# chop suey

/tʃɔp suːiː/ *adj., n.*

**Source language:** Cantonese (雜碎).

**Definition:** ❶ an adjective describing mixed ethnic

backgrounds; ❷ an adjective describing a diffuse mixture; ❸ a type of food traditionally made with meat and organ scraps (obscure in HKE, but common in other English-speaking countries).

**Text example:**

❶ "She'd also told him that the local Cantonese expression for Eurasian was a derogatory equivalent of '**chop suey** breed.'"

❷ "The cast of ministers, princes, courtiers and peasants are a motley gang clothed in an assortment of *faux chinoiserie*, costumes covering all dynasties and ranks, **chop suey** style, and it is impossible for knowledgeable viewers not to laugh."

❸ "This game differs as much from the American version as Chinese **chop suey** from the American dish." ★★★★☆

# chow-chow

/tʃaʊ tʃaʊ/ *n.*

**Source language:** Chinese Pidgin English.

**Definition:** ❶ mixed preserved food (archaic); ❷ mixed cargo (archaic).

**Text example:**

❶ "Dear me, I had no idea that the Chinese had such a variety of **chow-chow**. The fact is, I have not by any means exhausted my list of street cries of this nature. The Cantonese are gourmands and they pride themselves on their art of cooking."

❷ "A '**chow-chow**' cargo is an assorted cargo; a general shop is a '**chow-chow**' shop." ★☆☆☆☆

# chow fan

/tʃaʊ faːn/ *n.*

**Source language:** Cantonese (炒飯).

**Definition:** fried rice.

**Text example:**

"You may have been to tons of dim sum restaurants, you may have tried mooncakes, you may also have had more **chow fan** (fried rice) and chow mein (fried noodles) than you can handle."

# chow mein

/tʃaʊ miːn/ *n.*
**Source language:** Cantonese (炒麵).
**Definition:** fried noodles.

See: **chow fan**.

**Note:** There is an often erroneous opinion held in the West that *chow mein* is not eaten in China and that the practice of frying noodles originated in North America. The HKE pronunciation for the "ei" in this word is /iː/, whereas outside of HK /eɪ/ is more common.

# Christian

*n.*
**Definition:** a Protestant.
**Text example:**

"In Hong Kong the Protestants try to reserve **Christian** for themselves, and have had some success in influencing everyday usage. People who should know better will reply to the question 'Is he a **Christian**' with 'No, he is a Catholic.'"

# chuk kam

/tʃʌk kʌm/ *n.*
**Source language:** Cantonese (足金).
**Definition:** nearly pure gold, not less than 990 parts per thousand.
**Text example:**

"The standards of fineness ... are: Standard Fineness, not

less than 8 carat 333; 9 carat 375; 12 carat 500; 14 carat 585; 15 carat 625; 18 carat 750; 22 carat 916.6; **Chuk Kam** 990; and so in proportion for any other number of carats."

**Note:** Prior to 2008 the standard was 990 parts per thousand. It has been changed to 999 parts per thousand.

# Chung Yeung Festival

/tʃən jən/ *n.*

**Source languages:** Cantonese (重陽節), English.

**Definition:** a statutory holiday on the ninth day of the ninth lunar month, for cleaning ancestors' graves.

**Text example:**

"The 'Double Ninth' was originally the Day for Climbing the Hills, the festival when all good Chinese believed they must visit high places. Today, the pragmatic Cantonese combine it with the **Ch'ung Yeung**—the Autumn Festival, when ancestral graves are visited, swept clean, and offerings placed graves."

# Chuppies

See: **Chippies**.

# circulating libraries

*fixed expression.*

**Definition:** a business where a person carries a collection of rentable books from house to house (archaic).

**Text example:**

"I have often heard of '**circulating libraries**'; but before I reached this country I never saw them carried through the streets so as to accommodate every man at his own door."

**Note:** It is the library itself, rather than just the books, which is circulating.

# civet cat

*n.*

**Definition:** a long-tailed mammal of the species *Paguma larvata*.

**Text example:**

> "Antibody-dependent conformational changes have previously been reported for a **civet cat** strain of SARS-CoV which showed enhanced entry into a human renal epithelial cell-line in the presence of human monoclonal antibodies against human strain of SARS-CoV Spike."

See: **palm civet**.

**Note:** Outside of HKE this animal is more commonly called musang. It is known in HK for its link to SARS.

# Co-hong

*n.*

**Source language:** Chinese Pidgin English.

**Definition:** an organization of Chinese merchants in nineteenth-century Canton who monopolized business with European merchants (archaic).

**Text example:**

> "The **Co-hong** (kitng-hang) was a guild organized in 1720 by the hong merchants of Kwangtung and Fukien. It adopted a code of thirteen articles to regulate trade at Canton. After 1782, its members controlled the foreign trade at Canton altogether."

See: **hong**.

# compensated dating

*fixed expression.*

**Definition:** a form of prostitution based on an escort service.

**Text example:**

> "Girls as young as 15 are providing sex services using the

internet to advertise themselves as available for so-called '**compensated dating**', according to social workers."

# comprador (also compradore)

/kɔmprəˈdɔə(r)/ /kɔmprəˈdɜːr/ *n.*

**Source language:** Indian English.

**Definition:** a Chinese man who was responsible for relations between European merchants and the Chinese community (archaic).

**Text example:**

❶ "He was also a **comprador** and a very successful businessman."

❷ "The **Compradore** of the ship (i.e., the person in charge of the Chinese crew and trade with the Chinese) very kindly lent us his cabin as well, while he doubled up somewhere else."

# compradore account

*n.*

**Definition:** a company financial account where an employee could withdraw from their future salary (obscure and archaic).

**Text example:**

"We had a magic thing called the '**compradore account**', and whenever you wanted some money you went down to the basement of the office, to a little cash counter, signed a chit, and somebody gave you the money. At the end of the month it was knocked off your salary."

See: **comprador**.

# compradorship

*n.*

**Definition:** the state of being a comprador (obscure and archaic).

**Text example:**

"After father retired, because of poor health, from the **compradorship** of Messrs. Jardine, Matheson and Company, Uncle Ho Fook was appointed to the position and remained there until he retired several decades later."

See: **comprador**.

# **Confucius (孔子), Birthday of**

*n.*

**Definition:** a non-statutory holiday on the 27th day of the eighth month of the lunar calendar.

**Text example:**

"The major festival of Confucianism is the **birthday of Confucius** which falls on the 27th day of the eighth moon. Confucians in Hong Kong have always been deeply involved in education. They run a number of schools locally with the objective of promoting the teachings of Confucius."

# **congee**

/kɔndʒiː/ *n.*

**Source language:** Indian English.

**Definition:** a thick rice porridge (often with meat or fried bread added).

**congee** (photo by P. J. Cummings)

**Text example:**

"Generally, boil the water first, then put in the rice, cook it over 'wu fire' (quick and strong heat) until it is on the boil, then switch to 'wen fire' (slow and low heat) until the soup of the **congee** boiled away to well-done."

See: **boat/sampan congee, juk**.

# coolie (also cooly)

/ˈkuːliː/ *n.*

**Source language:** Indian English.

**Definition:** a hired laborer or porter (largely archaic).

**Text example:**

Current use:

❶ "Where Sellers contract to supervise erection of Machines, it shall be understood that all necessary **coolie** labor, lifting or hoisting tackle, materials for foundations, or supports, etc., shall be supplied and paid for by Buyer(s)."

Archaic use:

❷ "**Coolies** moved to Western District for work, and Kennedy Town was developed to settle people."

❸ "A servant or hired **cooly** thereupon carries a bucket full of the water to the house."

**Note:** *Coolie* is still used to describe unskilled labor. However, today this term may be considered patronizing or offensive.

# copy

*adj.*

**Definition:** an adjective describing an item without legal intellectual property rights.

**Text example:**

"This is not a **copy** DVD box set it's the real deal."

# crossed cheque

*n.*

**Definition:** a banking check which has two parallel lines drawn across the upper left-hand corner. Such a check will only be deposited in the receiver's bank account and the bearer will not be paid in cash.

**Text example:**

"Payment can be made by **Crossed Cheque** payable to 'Mouth & Foot Painting Artists Limited.'"

**Note:** The practice of crossing a check is an international convention, and the term is not exclusive to HK. However, as compared to, e.g., British English, it is far more frequently used in HKE (see: Introduction).

# cross-strait

*adj.*

**Definition:** relating to relationships between Taiwan and Mainland China, across the Taiwan Straits.

**Text example:**

"After the ground-breaking Mainland visits by Kuomintang and People First Party last year, yesterday's announcement signified that the **cross-strait** relations could be further strengthened."

# cumshaw

/kʌmʃɔː/ *n.*

**Source language:** Chinese Pidgin English.

**Definition:** a bribe or gratuity.

**Text example:**

"However, as usual, a **cumshaw** (bribe) smoothed away the objections."

# D

# D

*abbreviation.*

**Definition:** drugs or its consumption.

**Text example:**

"**D**: 1. drugs 2. having taken drugs."

# dai jap hai

/daɪ dʒaːp haɪ/ *idiomatic expression.*

**Source language:** Cantonese (大閘蟹).

**Definition:** an investor locked into an investment.

**Text example:**

"People are still cautious, or they are **Dai Jap Hai** waiting to be released."

**Note:** This use is motivated by the original sense common in Cantonese "a hairy crab served tied up."

# dai pai dong

/daɪ paɪ dɔŋ/ *n.*

**Source language:** Cantonese (大牌檔).

**Definition:** a street restaurant (often for the working class).

**Text example:**

"But if you're on a budget it's worthwhile exploring the **dai pai dongs**, the cheap street stall from which you can buy excellent food for just a few dollars."

# dan tat (also daan tat)

/daːn taːt/ *n.*

**Source language:** Cantonese (蛋撻).

**Definition:** egg tart.

**Text example:**

❶ "The egg tarts ('**dan tat**') are freshly baked on location throughout the day."

❷ "For a side dish, there's hot sweet buns stuffed with melted butter called *bor lau bau*, a tasty egg custard **daan tat** or the straight doughnut *yau char gwai*."

# DB

See: **Discovery Bay**.

# D-Bay

See: **Discovery Bay**.

# dim sum

/dim sʌm/ *n.*

**Source language:** Cantonese (點心).

**Definition:** a variety of different traditional Cantonese foods usually of a size to be picked up by chopsticks. Examples include *har gow* and *shaomai*.

**Text example:**

"They ordered a tea, and a steamer basket of tripe, the only **dim sum** the kitchen had left."

**Note:** The spelling *tim sum* is obscure in HKE, but more common in Singapore.

# dim sum house

*n.*

**Definition:** a restaurant where dim sum is eaten.

**Text example:**

"Yau Ma Tei is where you will find this lost world of Hong Kong: a **dim sum house** where you can have your lunch and then while away the afternoon hours between 2.30 and five every weekday."

# Discovery Bay, DB, D-Bay, Disco Bay

*n.*

**Definition:** an expatriate residential area. It is often seen as culturally isolated from the Hong Kong Chinese community.

# djunk

/dʒʌnk/ *n.*
See: **junk**.

# do-jeh

/dɔ dʒə/ *interjection.*
**Source language:** Cantonese (多謝).
**Definition:** an expression equivalent to "thank you," but used only for a gift or a compliment, but not for a service (usually spoken language).
**Text example:**

"Thank you for coming to our concerts and supporting us locals! It means a lot to us. **Do Jeh**."

# domestic helper

*fixed expression.*
**Definition:** a person who works within the employer's home doing household chores.
**Text example:**

"A Filipina **domestic helper** said, 'I really don't know why Hong Kong people are so crazy about that. In other countries there is panic-buying of rice.'"

# Double Ninth

*n.*
See: **Chung Yeung Festival**.

# Double Tenth

*n.*

**Definition:** ❶ anniversary of the rebellion against the last Chinese dynasty; ❷ a failed ceasefire agreement between the Kuomintang (KMT) and Communist Party.

**Text example:**

❶ "1911 Mutiny of Imperial troops at Wuchang on 10 October ('**Double Tenth**') leads to the outbreak of Chinese Revolution and the declaration of a republic at Nanking."

❷ "The failure of the Marshall mission was in fact a foregone conclusion. Equally the earlier-made **Double Tenth** Agreement (through Hurley's efforts) for ceasefire among the KMT and the CCP proved to be hollow."

# doubling-down

*fixed expression.*

**Definition:** Acting on a junior post in addition to one's own (e.g., in the Civil Service).

**Text example:**

"Acting allowance should not be granted for **doubling-down** acting appointment (i.e., a senior officer taking on the job of a junior officer in addition to his own)."

# doubling-sideways

*fixed expression.*

**Definition:** Acting on a post at the same rank in addition to one's own post (e.g., in the Civil Service).

**Text example:**

"Doubling-up, **doubling-sideways** or doubling-down. The acting appointment is for an officer to undertake the duties of a post in a higher, same or lower rank, in addition to the duties of his own post."

## doubling-up

*fixed expression.*

**Definition:** acting on a post at a higher rank in addition to one's own post (e.g., in the Civil Service).

See: **acting-up**, **doubling-sideways**.

## dou fu fa

/daʊ fu: fa:/ *n.*

**Source language:** Cantonese (豆腐花).

**Definition:** a dessert made with soft tofu and served with sweet ginger syrup.

**Text example:**

"The other case concerned an old woman who did good business at a Tsuen Wan street corner selling bean curd dessert or **doufu fa**."

## Dragon Boat Festival

*n.*

See: **Tuen Ng**.

## drunken chicken

*n.*

**Definition:** a chicken dish where the meat has been marinated in alcohol.

**Text example:**

"There are also noted poultry dishes, like **drunken chicken**, flavored with liberal amounts of Shaoshing wine and served cold."

## duck

*n.*

**Definition:** a male prostitute.

See: **chick**.

# E

**Eastern District
elderlies
estate**

# Eastern District

*n.*

**Definition:** a district in the northeastern part of Hong Kong Island. ★★★★★

# elderlies

*n.*

**Definition:** elderly people.

**Text example:**

"The mortality rate and outcome of the **elderlies** are not affected by the availability of positive microbiology results." ★★★★☆

# estate

*n.*

**Definition:** an area of a city zoned for a single purpose often with one developer; Housing Estate, Industrial Estate.

**Text example:**

❶ "The **estate** is 'managed' centrally by the Housing Authority for a public housing **estate**, and a manager appointed according to the Deed of Mutual Covenant (DMC) for a private housing **estate**."

❷ "By 1980 there were 45 ha of serviced sites available in the Tai Po Industrial **Estate** and 29 land contracts had been signed." ★★★★☆

# F

face
Falun Gong
fan
fan gwei(lo)
Fanling
fan tan
fat choi
fen
feng shui
FILTH
foki
foreign mud
fruit money
fu mo kwun
fung shui

# face

*n.*

**Definition:** to lose, gain or save one's reputation.

**Text example:**

> "From the Confucian point of view ... a man in the workforce is equated with worth, diligence, controllability, and a conscience for himself, and more importantly, such a man has fulfilled the masculine social role and identity in which his family could gain **face** and support."

**Note:** ❶ In Standard English this term is always expressed in the sense of losing or saving face. In HKE face can be gained. ❷ The use of this word by HK Chinese has been stereotyped in some Western fictions.

# Falun Gong

/faːlun gɔŋ/ *n.*

**Source language:** Cantonese (法輪功).

**Definition:** a religious organization that is illegal in Mainland China.

**Text example:**

> "These images illustrate the dichotomy of **Falun Gong**: it presents a rational, non-threatening image to outsiders ... while a closer examination of the cult throws up weird and wacky theories and prophecies."

See: **qigong**.

# fan (1)

/faːn/ *n.*

**Source language:** Cantonese (飯).

**Definition:** rice.

**Text example:**

> "To eat **fan**, a diner raises the bowl to her lips and pushes the grains into her mouth with chopsticks. This is the

easiest way to eat it and shows proper enjoyment—
eating **fan** from a bowl left sitting on the table suggests
dissatisfaction with the food."

# fan (2)

/fʌn/ *n.*
**Source language:** Cantonese (分).
**Definition:** ❶ 1/1600 catty or 1 candareen; ❷ 10 fan
(candareen) = 1 tsin (mace).

See: **catty**.

# fan (3)

/fʌn/ *n.*
**Source language:** Cantonese (分).
**Definition:** 0.371475 centimeters.

See: **chek**.

# fan gwei(lo) (also fanqui, fan kwai, fan-kwei)

/fan gweɪ (ləʊ)/ *idiomatic expression.*
**Source language:** Cantonese (番鬼佬).
**Definition:** literally, "troublesome ghost" (possibly
offensive), a derogatory name for Caucasian.
**Text example:**

❶ "They are still 'foreign devils' to the locals, but the term
**fan gweilo** or simply *gweilo* is usually uttered in a neutral,
ironic, or even an indulgent way, and hardly ever in tones
of fear and loathing."

❷ "This proved so popular that we had to arrange a second
crew, and we called ourselves by the irreverent names of
'**fan gwei**' for the mainly police and army crew and 'gweilo'
for the civilian team—two common abbreviations for '**fan
gweilo**' or foreign devils."

❸ "... and to carry a **fanqui** (foreign devil) to whampoa."

❹ "Magistrate: Did not that witness say **fan kwai** in his evidence?"

❺ "and the children cried '**Fan-kwei**' again, after me—even the smallest shrimps and mudlarks of two years old."

See: **gweilo**.

**Note:** Derived from the term *gweilo* and the Cantonese word for "trouble" (*mah-faahn*).

# Fanling

/fanliŋ/ *n.*

**Source language:** Cantonese (粉嶺).

**Definition:** a growing market town in the North District. It is the site of some old walled villages.

# fan tan

/fan tan/ *n.*

**Source language:** Cantonese (番攤).

**Definition:** a betting game based on the number of counters remaining when a hidden pile of them has been divided by four.

**Text example:**

"This analysis is based on the 1347 gamblers without missing data and the result is similar to 2001 in terms of the gambling related risk factors (Casino is replaced by **Fan Tan** and Mahjong House), and education is replaced by family income as a demographic risk factor."

# fat choi (also fat choy)

/fat tʃɔɪ/ *n.*

**Source language:** Cantonese (發財).

**Definition:** a soft stringy food (of the species *Nostoc commune* var. *Flagelliforme*) often served at Chinese New Year.

**Text example:**

❶ "We should share our responsibility and not eat **fat choi** to avoid damaging the soil and earth."

❷ "Foods play a prominent role in Hong Kong superstitions, from eating noodles on birthdays (long strands symbolize longevity), using **fat choy** (sea moss) as a prosperity-propitious ingredient in dishes, or using peach pits as amulets for babies."

**Note:** ❶ This term is a homophone for "get rich" in Cantonese. ❷ Many people mistakenly call this bacterial food a sea moss or fungi.

# fen

/fen/ *n.*

**Source language:** Mandarin (分).

**Definition:** Chinese currency, equivalent to one hundredth of a yuan Renminbi.

**Text example:**

"Currency: The currency unit since 1955 has been the Yuan, known as Renminbi (people's currency!). 1 Yuan Renminbi (¥ Rmb) = 10 *jiao* = 100 **fen**."

See: **Renminbi** and **jiao**.

# feng shui

/fəŋ ʃɔɪ/ *n.*

See: **fung shui**.

# FILTH

*idiomatic expression.*

**Definition:** acronym for "failed in London try Hong Kong," for those seeking to improve their prospects in the (former) colony.

**Text example:**

"Laura had assumed from the accent that Edie was

Oxbridge, but she was actually **FILTH**: Failed In London, Try Hong Kong."

# foki

/ˈfɔki/ *n.*
**Source language:** Cantonese (伙記).
**Definition:** ❶ co-worker (archaic); ❷ waiter (archaic).
**Text example:**

❶ "The 1st respondent telephoned the 2nd respondent and said he found the work not suitable for himself but that he would get a '**foki**' to take a look and submit a quotation (so that the ironwork might be sub-contracted by the 2nd respondent to the '**foki**')."

❷ "When a **foki** (waiter), Law Lau, reached the corridor, he saw Grandfather injured, holding on to the wall, and looking very pale. Instead of stopping to help, he followed a man in white trousers and a short jacket who darted through the passage from the Club."

# foreign mud

*idiomatic expression.*
**Definition:** opium.
**Text example:**

"In the 1830s imports of 'foreign mud' (a Chinese epithet for opium) almost trebled, reaching an astonishing 40,000 chests annually."

# fruit money

*fixed expression.*
**Definition:** old age or disability welfare payment by the government.
**Text example:**

"The residency requirements for disability and old age or retirement assistance (locally called 'fruit money' as the HK$700 [US$90] per month stipend is enough to do little more than buy fruit) fell somewhere between the requirements for housing and CSSA, at three to five years."

# fu mo kwun

/fuː məʊ guːn/ *n.*

**Source language:** Cantonese (父母官).

**Definition:** a traditional Imperial Chinese magistrate or official (archaic).

**Text example:**

"The New Territories Administration was encouraged in this attitude by the common people who from time immemorial have addressed the local officials as **fu mo kwun** ('father and mother officers')."

**Note:** Appointments were continued for a while by the British colonial government.

# fung shui

/fəŋ ʃɔɪ/ *n.*

**Source language:** Cantonese (風水).

**Definition:** a Chinese belief system based on surrounding effects of wind and water.

**Text example:**

"The Barclays Bank people in Hong Kong have just moved house. Like all well-assimilated foreign firms in Hong Kong, they called in a **fung shui** expert to advise them on whether they needed to install goldfish, mirrors, trees, waterfalls, crispy-fried roast piglets, etc."

**Note:** In Standard English, the spelling is *feng shui* and the pronunciation differs.

gai lan
gaylo
gei wai
General Kwan
ghost
godown
golden lily feet
Golden Mountain
golden rice bowl
grand chop

# G

Grave Sweeping Festival
green hat
griffin
grinding bean curd
guanxi
gung hei fat choy
gwai jai
gwai mui
gwaipoh
Gwan Yu
gweilo

# gai lan

/gaɪ laːn/ *n.*

**Source language:**
Cantonese (芥蘭).

**Definition:** a leafy vegetable
of the species *Brassica
oleracea* var. *alboglabra*.

**Text example:**

"Scallops were pretty fresh
and the **gai lan** (Chinese
broccoli) was pretty tasty.
This was our 'vegetable'
dish of the night."

★★★★★

**gai lan** (drawing by Adrian
Cennydd Petyt)

# gaylo

/geɪləʊ/ *idiomatic expression.*

**Source languages:** English, Cantonese (基佬).

**Definition:** a homosexual man.

**Text example:**

"YongSik and Eddie bought me another turtle called
Pooh-Pooh and YS made sure it was female cos if Piggy
was male, they could have S*X, if piggy was female 'at least
lesbo is better than **gaylo**, right.'"

★★★☆☆

# gei wai

/geɪ waɪ/ *n.*

**Source language:** Cantonese (基圍).

**Definition:** ❶ shrimp raised in coastal ponds; ❷ the
pond itself.

**Text example:**

"The Tour takes visitors through a variety of wildlife
habitats. First are Hong Kong's last traces of the
traditionally operated shrimp ponds (called **gei wai**),

which use fresh water from the Shenzhen River estuary to rear fish and shrimps." ⭐⭐⭐⭐

# General Kwan (also Gwan Yu)

/kwaːn -/ /gwaːn juː/ *n.*

**Source language:** Cantonese (關公/關帝).

**Definition:** an iconic figure who was a historical general under warlord Liu Bei during the late Eastern Han dynasty and Three Kingdoms. He played a significant role in the civil war that led to the collapse of the Han dynasty and the establishment of the Kingdom of Shu, of which Liu Bei was the first emperor. General Kwan is still worshiped in Hong Kong for his virtue.

**Text example:**

"Paintings, statues and other likenesses of **General Kwan** can be found in almost every traditional Shaolin kung fu school. Many government offices, police stations and post offices also display images of **General Kwan**, for his symbolic representation of righteousness, loyalty, humbleness and justice." ⭐⭐⭐⭐⭐

**General Kwan** (photo by P. J. Cummings)

# ghost

*n.*

**Definition:** a(n) (ancestral) spirit.

**Text example:**

> "The older **ghosts** may enjoy watching Chinese opera, but times have changed and the younger generation of '**ghosts**' like watching this type of performance."

**Underlying conceptualizations:** A SUPERNATURAL BEING IS A HUMAN BEING, A DECEASED MEMBER OF THE COMMUNITY IS A SUPERNATURAL BEING [TARGET DOMAIN ➡ DECEASED MEMBERS OF THE COMMUNITY] [SOURCE DOMAIN ➡ SUPERNATURAL BEING].

# godown

/gəʊdaʊn/ *n.*

**Source languages:** Malay, Indian English.

**Definition:** a building for the storage of goods and supplies.

**Text example:**

> "As merchants were no longer required to keep large stocks, some of the **godowns** in Eastern District were closed."

**Note:** The word comes from the Malay *gadong* for store-room, by way of Indian English. It is in common use today, but appears to be slowly being replaced by the Standard English equivalent word "warehouse."

# golden lily feet

*idiomatic expression.*

**Definition:** bound feet of a wealthy Chinese woman (archaic).

**Text example:**

> "Their chief pride evidently centred in their poor little **'golden lily' feet**, reduced to the tiniest hoof in proof

of their exalted station. Of course, the so-called foot is little more than just the big toe, enclosed in a dainty wee shoe, which peeps out from beneath the silk-embroidered trousers."

# Golden Mountain

*idiomatic expression.*

**Definition:** ❶ the United States of America; ❷ California (both largely archaic).

**Text example:**

❶ "It was around that time that he heard stories about the fortunes being made in the new land across the seas, through building railroads or panning for gold. He decided to head for Hong Kong to earn his passage to the **Golden Mountain**."

❷ "The area was notorious for being poverty-stricken prior to the twentieth century, and there was a folk saying: 'If you want to prosper, go to the **Golden Mountain** (California).'"

# golden rice bowl

*idiomatic expression.*

**Definition:** a secure high paying job.

**Text example:**

"'With the higher salaries and better fringe benefits, a policeman's job is a **golden rice bowl** for me,' said Wong Chun-kit, who has an overseas diploma."

**Underlying conceptualization (generic):** A JOB IS A FOOD CONTAINER [TARGET DOMAIN ➡ OCCUPATION] [SOURCE DOMAIN ➡ FOOD CONTAINER].

See: **iron rice bowl**.

# grand chop

*fixed expression.*

**Definition:** a ship's port clearance permit (archaic).

**Text example:**

"The Hoppo finally delivered his '**grand chop**' once his officers had established that all dues had been paid—port entry tax ('ship measurement'), import and export duties, and all official payments to the pilots, to the compradors, to the linguists, and to the hong merchants."

See: **chop**.

★★★★★

# Grave Sweeping Festival

*n.*

See: **Ching Ming**, **Chung Yeung**.

★★☆☆☆

# green hat

*idiomatic expression.*

**Definition:** to have an unfaithful spouse.

**Text example:**

"If you don't want to make real relationship changes, i.e. more time and attention for her or more romance etc. Then cut that **green hat** tossing bitch out of your life like a cancer."

★★★★☆

# griffin

*n.*

**Definition:** ❶ a new race horse (colloquial); ❷ a Westerner new to Asia (archaic).

**Text example:**

❶ "The grass **griffin** trials originally set to be held on Tuesday 16 October 2001 at Sha Tin have been re-scheduled to Tuesday 9 October 2001. Privately Purchased Horses (PP's) which have not started in a race in Hong Kong are also eligible to enter."

❷ "**Griffin** was the name ... given to the wild pony imported from North China and used for horse racing in Shanghai,

Hong Kong and the Treaty Ports. The term '**griffin**' was thus applied to the untrained young European when he arrived in China to take up work with a foreign firm."

# grinding bean curd

*idiomatic expression.*

**Definition:** genital contact between lesbians.

**Text example:**

"Sexual practices like genital contact called '**grinding bean curd**.'"

# guanxi

/gwaːn ʃiː/ /kwaːn ʃiː/ *n.*

**Source language:** Mandarin (關係).

**Definition:** business connections and relationships, often corrupt.

**Text example:**

"Confucius said 'gentleman wanting to be successful himself, helps others to be successful,' and that is the basic principle of **Guanxi**, the system of connections and reciprocal favours and mutual backscratching whereby Chinese give each other a hand to get one ahead, sidestepping the law legitimately where it is in the way."

# gung hei fat choy

/gɔŋ heɪ faːt ʃɔɪ/ *fixed expression.*

See: **kung hei fat choy**.

# gwai jai

/gwaɪ dʒaɪ/ /gweɪ dʒaɪ/ *n.*

**Source language:** Cantonese (鬼仔).

**Definition:** a Caucasian boy or child (possibly derogatory, literally "ghost child").

**Text example:**

"Dun be shy in front of your **gwai jai** friends and just have fun! hope u'll enjoy the night."

# gwai mui

/gwaɪ mɔɪ/ /gweɪ mɔɪ/ *n.*

**Source language:** Cantonese (鬼妹).

**Definition:** a young Caucasian female (possibly derogatory, literally "ghost girl").

**Text example:**

"I don't know, lots of **gwai mui**, to me, are very slutty. Not to say that there aren't any nice **gwai mui**, but we all know that none of our parents would want a **gwai mui**, because they don't respect their in-laws."

# gwaipoh (also gweipo, gwaipo, gwaipor)

/gwaɪ pə/ /gweɪ pəʊ/ *n.*

**Source language:** Cantonese (鬼婆).

**Definition:** a Caucasian female (possibly derogatory, literally "ghost woman").

**Text example:**

❶ "We've got to stop that **gwaipoh**!"

❷ Not suffering from yellow fever? Here's a **gweipo** version."

❸ "Her wedding had been all about that banquet, with the eyes of the whole Tang family on her, waiting for her to make a mistake so that they could say, *you can't expect a* **gwaipo** *to know our customs*."

❹ "Just then, there was a knock at the door, and a red-haired **gwaipor** tentatively entered the room."

# Gwan Yu

/kwaːn –/ /gwaːn juː/ *n.*
**Source language:** Chinese name (關羽).

See: **General Kwan**.

# gweilo (also gwailo)

/gwaɪ ləʊ/ /gweɪ ləʊ/ *n.*
**Source language:** Cantonese (鬼佬).
**Definition:** a Caucasian male (possibly derogatory, literally "ghost man").

**Text example:**

❶ "The area has survived tragedy, seen off competition, and beaten its reputation for being a '**gweilo** ghetto' to become an international entertainment hub with even bigger designs on the future."

❷ "Inside he found a queue of three other **gwailo**—two Americans and an Englishman—all of whom had the same brief sojourn in China."

See: **gwaipoh**, **gwai mui**, **gwai jai**.

**Note:** *Kwai-lo* in Malaysian English.

haam daan
ha gao
hairy gourd
hak gwai
Hakka
hand tail
har gow
hasma soup
haw fun
hell
hell money
heung cheung
heung ha

# H

hill fire
hit airplane
HKSAR Establishment Day
hoey
hoisin sauce
hong
hong-boat
Hongcouver
Hongkie
Hongkonger
Hongkongeress
Hong Kong Flu
Hong Kong foot
Hong Kong Island
Honkers
house-coolie
H share
hui
hundred-year-old egg
Hungry Ghost Festival

# haam daan

/haːm daːn/ *n.*

**Source language:** Cantonese (鹹蛋).

**Definition:** salted preserved egg.

**Text example:**

"**Haam daan** (salted eggs) are soaked in brine for about 40 days. This process causes the yolk to harden and turn orange. Unlike preserved eggs, these must be cooked. They might be broken into a dish of stir-fried tofu or fried rice, or hardboiled and chopped up into a bowl of juk."

# ha gao

/haː gaʊ/ *n.*

See: **har gow**.

# hairy gourd

*n.*

**Definition:** a hairy immature winter melon used in cooking.

**Text example:**

"Lillian Lee relishes the **hairy gourd** cooked with dried shrimps and rice vermicelli, while old Mrs Lee ... is so fond of fatty pork stewed with yam that she has eaten almost half the plate herself."

**Note:** Also called *hairy melon* and *wax gourd* outside of HK.

# hak gwai (also hak gwei)

/haːk gwaɪ/ *n.*

**Source language:** Cantonese (黑鬼).

**Definition:** a dark skinned person (derogatory).

**Text example:**

❶ "They just kept referring to us as **hak gwai** (black devil) among themselves and said to me 'you visitors come to Hong Kong to beat up a Hong Kong Man.'"

❷ "Their response was unanimous: 'How can a **hak-gwei** [meaning 'black devil'] become president of the United States?' Other remarks were a bit too caustic to publish."

★★★☆☆

# Hakka

/haːkaː/ *n.*

**Source language:** Hakka (客家).

**Definition:** a Chinese ethnic group.

**Text example:**

"Here we see A's reasons for why Hakka cuisine became popular in the 1950s and 1960s, as well as how and why the nearby **Hakka** restaurants in Hong Kong have declined during the last two decades."

★★★★★

# hand tail

*idiomatic expression.*

**Source language:** Cantonese (手尾).

**Definition:** a leftover task.

**Text example:**

"Tomorrow will be my last day of work in HKEAA, I wish to take this opportunity to wish you all have a MERRY CHRISTMAS and a HAPPY NEW YEAR! Should you wish to contact me in future, no matter is to clear '**HAND TAILS**' or to join your activities, you can call my mobile—or email me at—."

★★☆☆☆

# har gow (also har gau, ha gao, har kow)

/haː gaʊ/ *n.*

**Source language:** Cantonese (蝦餃).

**Definition:** a prestige variety of dim sum, consisting of a starch envelope and shrimp stuffing.

**Text example:**

❶ "There are many dim sum specialties to choose from, 10 from the main menu and about the same from a menu offering specialties. We loaded up on the obligatory **har gow** and siu mai."

❷ "Martin Yan learns how to prepare **har gau** and other varieties of dim sum."

❸ "**Ha gao**—shrimps, bamboo shoots, and flavouring enclosed in a purse of semi-translucent rice flour and water paste,"

❹ "And it is impossible to buy the translucent dough made from wheat starch for making Shrimp Dumplings (**Har Kow**)." ★★★★☆

**har gaw** (photo by P. J. Cummings)

# hasma soup

/ˈhasmɔ suːp/ *n.*

**Source language:** Mandarin (雪蛤膏).

**Definition:** a sweet soup of frog reproductive organs.

**Text example:**

"The **hasma soup** served at Heng Fa Low is a good example. It's made with tapioca pearls and bits of this and that, and it comes either hot or cold, but it's always sweet. And it's fortified with the sperm of a Chinese tree frog." ★★☆☆☆

# haw fun

/hɔ: fʌn/ *n.*

**Source language:** Cantonese (河粉).

**Definition:** a flat broad rice noodle.

**Text example:**

"**Haw fan** are wide, white, flat, slippery rice noodles, and are usually pan fried."

# hell

*n.*

**Definition:** the traditional Daoist underworld.

**Text example:**

"The Great Emperor of Fengdu ranked in the highest class of spirits in **hell**. In charge of all affairs of **hell**, he was known as the king of spirits. After people died, they went to **hell**. Their souls would be judged by the King of Spirits."

**Note:** The meaning of this term differs from the Christian and Muslim understanding of "hell."

# hell money (also hell bank notes)

*n.*

See: **spirit money**.

# heung cheung

/hʌŋ tʃʌŋ/ *n.*

**Source language:** Cantonese (鄉長).

**Definition:** a village head (archaic, obscure).

**Text example:**

"A week later, the **heung cheung**, or village head, of O Mun came to see me in Kowloon."

# heung ha

/hʌŋ ha:/ *n.*

**Source language:** Cantonese (鄉下).

**Definition:** ancestral village or home town, often in Mainland China.

**Text example:**

"You should see my **heung ha**—my ancestral village in China."

# hill fire

*n.*

**Definition:** similar to bush fire or forest fire, but of more common usage in Hong Kong.

**Text example:**

"A **hill fire** at Pat Sin Leng Country Park took the lives of teachers and students and seriously injured others from Fung Yiu King Secondary School in Ma On Shan."

# hit airplane

*idiomatic expression.*

**Definition:** male masturbation.

**Text example:**

"Either **hit the airplane** less often, or get a more attractive gf."

# HKSAR Establishment Day

*n.*

**Definition:** statutory holiday on July 1, starting in 1997, the date of the handover of HK from the British.

**Text example:**

"Notably they are rather indifferent toward the celebration of the National Day (October 1) or the **HKSAR Establishment Day** (July 1), though the extra holidays are welcome by most people."

See: **July 1**.

# hoey

/hɔɪ/ *n.*
See: **hui**.

# hoisin sauce

/hɔɪsin sɔːs/ *n.*
**Source language:** Cantonese (海鮮醬).
**Definition:** a seafood sauce also used for other products.
**Text example:**

> "**Hoisin Sauce**. This sweet, piquant brown paste is made from soybeans, red beans, sugar, garlic, vinegar, chilli, sesame oil and flour. It's an essential with Peking Duck."

# hong

/hɔŋ/ *n.*
**Source language:** Cantonese (行).
**Definition:** a large old foreign-owned Hong Kong business (largely archaic).
**Text example:**

> "But what does the future hold for the British **hongs**—Jardines and Swire prominent among them—after July 1997?"

See: **Co-hong**.

**Note:** This term is becoming archaic since there are no new *hongs*, even if a company is a large foreign business.

# hong-boat

*n.*
**Source language:** Cantonese.
**Definition:** a type of boat, with a small house, often used by European merchants in HK (archaic).

**Text example:**

"Here a **hong-boat**, gaily painted, was sent to take us on shore, where we were hospitably entertained by Mr. ----, in the house of the firm." ☆☆☆☆☆

# Hongcouver

*idiomatic expression.*

**Definition:** a slang term for Vancouver, Canada, because many people of Hong Kong descent reside there.

**Text example:**

"The only cheering thing this week was a speech from Hongkong's Banking Commissioner, Mr Tony Nicolle. He said that even if all the forex dealers flew off to **Hongcouver**, er, Vancouver, there would still be enough business to go around, because the Hongkong economy was buzzing along at a good rate." ★★★☆☆

# Hongkie (1)

*n.*

**Definition:** a slang term for a Hongkonger, usually used by Singaporeans (derogatory).

**Text example:**

"Does one really remember how many times a **hongkie** said thanks, please, or sorry?" ★★★☆☆

# Hongkie (2)

*n.*

**Definition:** a slang term for Hong Kong dollar, usually used by non-Hong Kong people.

**Text example:**

"Where's she going to find two thousand **Hongkies** for a mobile phone when she only makes fourteen a month?"

 ★★★☆☆

# Hongkonger (also **Hong Konger**)

*n.*

**Source language:** Cantonese (香港人), English.

**Definition:** the most common term for a person of Hong Kong origin or affiliation.

**Text example:**

❶ "Perhaps rather than describing yourselves as Chinese, some would prefer to tell me that you are a '**Hongkonger**.'"

❷ "**Hong Kongers** like to finish a meal with a sweet."

★★★★☆

# Hongkongeress

*n.*

**Definition:** a woman of Hong Kong origin or affiliation (obscure and possibly archaic).

**Text example:**

"She is, for example, forever meeting an interesting or an open or a clever woman and defining her as very much not a '**hongkongeress**.'"

★☆☆☆☆

# Hong Kong Flu

*n.*

**Definition:** a strain of influenza.

**Text example:**

"The Asian Flu and the **Hong Kong Flu** took more than 1.5 million lives and caused economic losses exceeding US$32 billion."

★★★★☆

# Hong Kong foot

*idiomatic expression.*

**Definition:** athlete's foot.

**Text example:**

"Do not wear nylon socks or plastic sports shoes if you are prone to fungal infection of the feet (**Hong Kong foot**)."

See: **Shanghai foot**.

★★★★☆

# Hong Kong Island

*n.*

**Source language:** Cantonese (香港島), English.

**Definition:** an island in the southern part of Hong Kong from which the city/SAR derived its name.

⭐⭐⭐⭐⭐

# Honkers

*n.*

**Definition:** a slang term for Hong Kong, usually used by non-Hong Kong people.

**Text example:**

"I am very happy to have lunch with you today and to be given this opportunity to talk about the future of my home Hong Kong, or '**Honkers**' as I've heard it referred to by some of my Antipodean acquaintances." ⭐⭐⭐

# house-coolie

*n.*

**Source language:** Indian English.

**Definition:** a household servant (archaic).

**Text example:**

"Immediately under the boy for indoor work is the '**house-coolie**', whose business it is to swab floors, polish grates, light fires, trim lamps, clean knives and boots and make himself generally useful about the house."

See: **coolie**.

⭐⭐⭐⭐⭐

# H share

*n.*

**Definition:** shares of companies incorporated in Mainland China, traded on the Hong Kong Stock Exchange.

**Text example:**

"In establishing a framework for **H share** listings for Chinese enterprises, the Securities and Futures Commission, the Stock Exchange of Hong Kong, and the Chinese authorities recognized that a sound regulatory framework was critical."

# hui (also **hoey**)

/hɔɪ/ *n.*

**Source language:** Cantonese (會).

**Definition:** formerly a secret organization in Chinese society, sometimes acting as a credit union (archaic).

**Text example:**

❶ "The **Hui** developed into some kind of credit union where people gathered to contribute to a fund at regular intervals and bidding was introduced to determine who would get the use of this fund in that period."

❷ "The **hoey** unites men more closely even than the sons of one father in a family."

# hundred-year-old egg

*n.*

See: **century egg**.

# Hungry Ghost Festival

*n.*

See: **Yue Lan**.

II
iron rice bowl
Islands District

# II

/aɪ aɪ/ *n.*

**Definition:** a common abbreviation for "illegal immigrant," used as a word.

**Text example:**

> "In a visit to the Marine Police yesterday, the delegation exchanged views with officers of the regional headquarters on anti-**II** measures and had a look on the sea routes that the illegal immigrants sneaked into Hong Kong."

# iron rice bowl

*idiomatic expression.*

**Definition:** a secure job from which it would be difficult to be dismissed.

**Text example:**

> "The government recognises that the '**iron rice bowl**' is not conducive to economic modernisation and has also sought to reform the welfare system so that the burden falls on its own shoulders."

**Underlying conceptualization (generic):** A JOB IS A FOOD CONTAINER [TARGET DOMAIN ➡ OCCUPATION] [SOURCE DOMAIN ➡ FOOD CONTAINER].

See: **golden rice bowl**.

# Islands District

*n.*

**Definition:** a district including Lantau Island and several other islands on the southern side of the Hong Kong SAR.

# J

Jardine Johnnies
jetso
jiao
John Company
jook
jo san
joss
joss house
joss paper
joss stick
juk
July 1st
junk
ju yug bao

# Jardine Johnnies

/dʒɑːdiːn dʒɔniːs/ *idiomatic expression.*
**Source language:** Royal Navy slang.
**Definition:** Scottish families of whom many members have employment at the Jardine's Hong.
**Text example:**

"The **Jardine Johnnies** have been branching out into new businesses. Jardine Strategic has taken a stake in Christian Dior, the handbags and posh perfume company which supplies many a tai tai."

# jetso

/dʒetsəʊ/ *n.*
**Source language:** Cantonese (著數).
**Definition:** a bargain or special discount.
**Text example:**

"**Jetso** Spending Offer, Promotional Offer will be coming soon."

# jiao

/dʒaʊ/ *n.*
**Source language:** Mandarin (角).
**Definition:** Chinese currency.
**Text example:**

"The standard unit of currency in China is the renminbi (RMB), also known as the yuan. The smaller units are the **jiao** and the fen. One yuan is equivalent to 10 **jiao**, and one **jiao** equals 10 fen."

See: **Renmimbi** and **yuan**.

# John Company

*idiomatic expression.*
**Source language:** Indian English.

**Definition:** a personification of the East India Company (archaic).

**Text example:**

"Of all foreigners the English arrived in the greatest numbers. The East India Company, or '**John Company**', established its headquarters in Macau, first on the Praia Grande, and then in the lovely house that is now the Camões Museum." ★★☆☆☆

# jook

/dʒʌk/ /dʒuk/ *n.*

See: **juk**, **congee**.

# jo san (also jo sun)

/dʒəʊ sən/ *interjection, n.*

**Source language:** Cantonese (早晨).

**Definition:** a greeting equivalent to "good morning."

**Text example:**

❶ "**Jo-san**, please take care and don't catch cold!"

❷ "The people we met on the trail were friendly, often offering a joyful '**Jo Sun**' as we passed them." ★★★☆☆

# joss

/dʒɔs/ *n.*

**Source languages:** Chinese Pidgin English, Portuguese.

**Definition:** religious luck associated with Daoist gods, and/or ancestors.

**Text example:**

"Around seven the next morning, the British were about to begin shelling the city when Chinese on the nearby fort's walls again waved white flags, but this time also bellowed Elliot's name 'as if he had been their protecting **joss**', according to Edward Belcher." ★★★★★

# joss house

*n.*

**Definition:** temple.

**Text example:**

"The temple was built in the late 1840s or early 50s, for by 1852 a Chinese man was recorded as 'carer of the **Joss House**' in a deed Smith cites." ★★★★

# joss paper

*n.*

**Definition:** ❶ paper with prayers written on them; ❷ replica cash and consumer goods made of paper for the purpose of burning as offering to God, gods, or ancestors in Chinese tradition.

**Text example:**

❶ "Each of these sticks carries an inscription: which he writes especially for the occasion and is then covered with lucky red **joss paper**."

❷ "During the Chinese festival, it is imperative for families to deposit 'money' in the Bank of Hell by burning **joss paper** for the benefit of their ancestors."

**Underlying conceptualizations:** A SUPERNATURAL BEING IS A HUMAN BEING, A PAPER MODEL IS A REAL OBJECT IN THE SUPERNATURAL WORLD [TARGET DOMAINS ➡ SUPERNATURAL BEING, PAPER MODEL] [SOURCE DOMAINS ➡ HUMAN BEING, OBJECT IN THE SUPERNATURAL WORLD].

See: **hell bank notes.** ★★★☆

# joss stick

*n.*

**Definition:** incense burned in a ritual offering to God, gods, or ancestors.

**Text example:**

"They passed many statues of gods and goddesses, **joss**

**sticks** that were still lit and scrolls with beautiful Chinese words on them."

**Underlying conceptualization:** A SMELL IS A VALUABLE OBJECT IN THE SUPERNATURAL WORLD [TARGET DOMAINS ➡ SUPERNATURAL BEING, SWEET SMELL] [SOURCE DOMAIN ➡ OBJECT IN THE SUPERNATURAL WORLD].

# juk (also jook)

/dʒʌk/ /dʒʊk/ *n.*
**Source language:** Cantonese (粥).
**Definition:** rice porridge.
**Text example:**
❶ "Congee rice porridge or **juk**."
❷ "Congee also called **jook** in Cantonese, is usually served for breakfast. It is often made with plain water and flavored with various toppings which are mixed into the gruel individually."

See: **congee**, which is the more common term in HKE.

# July 1st (also July First)

*n.*
**Definition:** statutory holiday, officially HKSAR Establishment Day.
**Text example:**
❶ "The June Fourth vigils in Victoria Park, the **July 1st** protest marches, and the orchestrated anti-WTO (World Trade Organization) confrontations by Korean ..."
❷ "The Chairman of the Democratic Party ... described the delay as shameful. He warned that it would cause more people to join the **July first** rally."

**Note:** This term is more often used in everyday speech than the formal term "HKSAR Establishment Day."

# junk (also djunk)

/dʒʌnk/ *n.*

**Source language:** Malay.

**Definition:** a Chinese-style boat.

**Text example:**

"There are 17,000 **junks** and such craft registered in Hong Kong ... You have only to watch the cargo **junks** on the waterfront for a few minutes to realize that **junks** are not just ships but homes."

**Note:** *Djunk* is an obscure and archaic spelling.

**junk** (drawing by Adrian Cennydd Petyt)

# ju yug bao

/dʒu: ju:k baʊ/ *n.*

**Source language:** Cantonese (豬肉包).

**Definition:** pork buns.

**Text example:**

"Then bring out a couple of dim sum specialities: ha gao (shrimp bonnets) and **ju yug bao** (pork buns)."

kaido
kaifong
kai lan
Kai Tak rules
kan
kang
kang kong
kit fat
kong kong
Kowloon
Kowloon City
Kowloon Tong
Kowloon Walled City
kowtow
kuk
kung hei fat choy
kung-so
Kwai Chung

# K

Kwai Tsing District
Kwun Tong

# kaido (ferry) (also kaito)

/gaɪdəʊ/ *n.*

**Source language:** Cantonese (街渡).

**Definition:** a small boat often used for a ferry service or short-distance marine transport.

**Text example:**

❶ "If time permits, visitors might like to board a local **kaido** ferry at the old pier for the short channel trip to Lantau Island's peaceful hilltop Trappist monastery."

❷ "Members of the public are advised that the '**Kaito**' ferry service between Tsing Lung Tau and Luk Keng will cease operation with effect from 13 July 2009."　　　⬚ ?

# kaifong

/kaɪfɔŋ/ *n.*

**Source language:** Cantonese (街坊).

**Definition:** ❶ a neighborhood and mutual aid association; ❷ the individuals engaged in such an association.

**Text example:**

❶ "Kan discussed the strong government encouragement of the **kaifong** movement during the 1950s, when voluntary organizations were needed to provide social welfare and engage in community development work, and the subsequent reduction of the government's financial support when its Social Welfare Department assumed greater responsibility for social welfare services."

❷ "The beat officer had to talk to the **kaifongs** (residents), if only to relieve boredom."　　　⭐⭐⭐⭐

# kai lan

*n.*

See: **gai lan**.

# Kai Tak rules

*n.*

**Definition:** an assumption that persons entering, or leaving, Hong Kong by way of Kai Tak Airport are not bound by the usual rules of marital fidelity and are required to keep the infidelities of others a secret.

**Text example:**

"Writing an article on a successful tour while maintaining the sanctity of the **Kai Tak rules** is always a tricky one."

**Note:** The potential term "Chek Lap Kok rules" has not gained significant circulation.

# kan

/gʌn/ *n.*

**Source language:** Cantonese (斤).

**Definition:** 1 catty.

**Text example:**

"About 70 **kan** of Tahitian pearls were sold, bringing in US$4.14 million."

See: **catty**.

# kang

/kaŋ/ *adj.*

**Source language:** Mandarin (炕).

**Definition:** a style of furniture.

**Text example:**

"Several of the cabinets, low chests and **kang** coffers on display feature the flat fronted form, raised on short stylised 'leopard' legs, that is often associated with Sha'anxi and Gansu provinces."

**kang-style furniture**
(photo by P. J. Cummings)

# kang kong

/kæŋ kɔːŋ/ *n.*

**Source language:** Philippine English.

**Definition:** a leafy vegetable of the species *Ipomoea aquatica*, that is grown in wet soil.

**Text example:**

> "Well, just because we were at Lamma Island, a small Island which produces fresh homemade shrimp paste, I decided to try it with a vegetable dish. So, we ordered Stir-fried **Kang Kong** with shrimp paste."

**kang kong** (drawing by Adrian Cennydd Petyt)

# kit fat

/kit fat/ *n.*

**Source language:** Cantonese (結髮).

**Definition:** a first or senior wife.

**Text example:**

> "'Are you your husband's **kit fat**?', I asked the first wife—a **kit fat** is the first wife a man takes, ranking senior to any other wife he may subsequently take."

# kong kong

/kɔŋ kɔŋ/ *n.*
**Source language:** Cantonese (公公).
**Definition:** maternal grandfather.

See: **po-po.**

# Kowloon

/kaʊluːn/ *n.*
**Source language:** Cantonese (九龍).
**Definition:** ❶ the city on the peninsula of land north of Victoria Harbour; ❷ the peninsula of land north of Victoria Harbour.
**Text example:**

❶ "The third term of the **Kowloon** City District Council (KCDC), with 27 District Council Members, came into being on 1 January 2008."

❷ "Hong Kong Island was transferred by the Treaty of Nanjing in 1842, **Kowloon** Peninsula by the Convention of Beijing in 1860, and the New Territories (consisting of a mainland area adjoining **Kowloon** and 235 adjacent islands) by a 99-year lease under the Second Convention of Beijing in 1898."

# Kowloon City

*n.*
**Source language:** Cantonese (九龍城).
**Definition:** ❶ the Eastern part of the Kowloon Peninsula that includes the former Walled City of Kowloon, Ma Tau Wai, Hung Hom, Ho Man Tin and To Kwa Wan; ❷ the Walled City of Kowloon.
**Text example:**

❶ "This may be related to the larger proportion of private sector accommodation in **Kowloon City** which makes the electorate relatively less susceptible to mass mobilization efforts than the public housing estates in Wong Tai Sin."

❷ "However, **Kowloon City** was to remain an anomaly with the government ambivalent about their authority to administer it like the rest of the territory."

See: **Kwun Tong**.

**Note:** This reference is only to the eastern part of the Kowloon Peninsula and does not mean the same as "Kowloon" or the "City of Kowloon."  ⭐⭐⭐⭐⭐

# Kowloon Tong

/kaʊluːn tɔŋ/ *n.*
**Source language:** Cantonese (九龍塘).
**Definition:** an area in New Kowloon south of Lion Rock.  ⭐⭐⭐⭐⭐

# Kowloon Walled City

*n.*
**Source language:** Cantonese (九龍城寨).
**Definition:** an area of the city of Kowloon which remained Chinese territory and outside UK jurisdiction; notorious for vice and crime; demolished in the 1980s and 1990s.

**Text example:**

"In 1993, the **Walled City** was reconstructed as the **Walled City** Park where many relics of historical value have been preserved."  ⭐⭐⭐⭐⭐

**Kowloon Walled City** (drawing by Adrian Cennydd Petyt)

# kowtow

/ˈkaʊtaʊ/ n., v.

**Source language:** Cantonese (叩頭) or Mandarin.

**Definition:** ❶ a finger-based method of saying "thank you" to the person serving tea; ❷ a form of Chinese bowing where the forehead is knocked on the floor to (a) God or an altar; (b) a political leader (archaic); ❸ a metaphor for political submission.

**Text example:**

❶ "After a person's cup is filled, that person may knock his bent index and middle fingers (or some similar variety of finger tapping) on the table to express gratitude to the person who served the tea."

❷ "The attendance of the elders and the gentry was compulsory, while those over sixty were invited as guests of honour. The **kowtow** and the three prostrations were in the order of the government officials first, then the gentry, then the elders, then whoever happened to be there."

❸ "Relations between Seoul and Washington have been tense at times under Roh, a progressive elected on a wave of anti-Americanism in December 2002 after he vowed never to **kowtow** to the United States."

**kowtow** (drawing by Adrian Cennydd Petyt)

# kuk

/kʌk/ *n.*

**Source language:** Cantonese (局).

**Definition:** an association or organization.

**Text example:**

"The main objective of the **Kuk** is to care for the young and protect the innocent. In the early days, the **Kuk** was primarily engaged in suppressing abduction of women and children and providing shelters and education for such victims. Over the century, the **Kuk** has gradually evolved into a diversified organization."

**Note:** Now this term is usually limited to the charitable group the Po Leung Kuk and the ethnic political group Heung Yee Kuk.

# kung hei fat choy

/guŋ heɪ fat tʃɔɪ/ /kuŋ heɪ fat tʃɔɪ/
*fixed expression.*

**Source language:** Cantonese (恭喜發財).

**Definition:** a traditional greeting during Chinese New Year. Literally: congratulations (on) getting rich.

**Text example:**

"An early but very heartfelt **Kung Hei Fat Choy** to all the readers of this Viewpoint column throughout the world. May the Year of the Dragon bring prosperity and happiness to you and your family."

See: **lai see**.

# kung-so

/kuŋ sɔ/ *n.*

**Source language:** Cantonese (公所).

**Definition:** a place, often a temple building, used as an unofficial court of law or meditation for Chinese in early Hong Kong (archaic).

**Text example:**

"The **kung-so** adjacent to the temple served as the court of justice for the Chinese in the early days." ⭐☆☆☆☆

# Kwai Chung

/kwaɪ tʃuŋ/ *n.*

**Source language:** Cantonese (葵涌).

**Definition:** an area in the southeastern New Territories and part of Kwai Tsing District. It has one of the largest and busiest port facilities in the world. ⭐⭐⭐⭐⭐

# Kwai Tsing District

/kwaɪ tsɪŋ 'dɪstrɪkt/ *n.*

**Source language:** Cantonese (葵青).

**Definition:** a district south of Tsuen Wan, it is a Chinese acronym for its component parts Kwai Chung and Tsing Yi Island. ⭐⭐⭐⭐⭐

# Kwun Tong

/kuːn tɔŋ/ *n.*

**Source language:** Cantonese (觀塘).

**Definition:** a district in the eastern part of the Kowloon Peninsula that includes the former Walled City of Kowloon, Ma Tau Wai, Hung Hom, Ho Man Tin, and To Kwa Wan.

**Text example:**

"The purpose of setting up this Homepage is to enhance your understanding of the **Kwun Tong** District Council and strengthen our communication."

See: **Kowloon City**. ⭐⭐⭐⭐⭐

lai cha
lai see
lakh
laliloon
Lamma Island
Lan Kwai Fong
Lantau Island
Lantern Festival
lap sap
lap sap chung
lap-sap yan/lo/po
leng mo
leung
li
li man fu
linchi
ling chih
Lion Rock
little brother
localization
lolita

# L

lo mei
lo mein
Lover's Day
lucky money

# lai cha

/laɪ tʃaː/ *n.*

**Source language:** Cantonese (奶茶).

**Definition:** milk tea.

**Text example:**

> "Please bring her a cup of **lai-cha**, hot, sweet—two spoonfuls of sugar." ★★★☆☆

# lai see

/laɪ siː/ *n.*

**Source language:** Cantonese (利是).

**Definition:** ❶ money given as a gift in a red envelope; ❷ a gift of money intended as a bribe.

**Text example:**

❶ "Children and young adults will find more money in their **lai see** packets this Lunar New Year, according to a survey."

❷ "Staff must not solicit 'Lai See' from any external business associates in any circumstances."

**Underlying conceptualization:** A BRIBE IS A GIFT [TARGET DOMAIN ➡ CORRUPTION] [SOURCE DOMAIN ➡ GIFT].

See: **lucky money, red packet.** ★★★★☆

**laisee** (drawing by Adrian Cennydd Petyt)

# lakh

/lak/ *n.*

**Source language:** Indian English.

**Definition:** 100,000.

**Text example:**

"With intent to buy **lakh** gallons of jet fuel from Hong Kong Airport and another **lakh** gallons from Manchester Airport ..."  ★★★☆☆

# laliloon

*n.*

**Source language:** unknown.

**Definition:** robber (archaic and obscure).

**Text example:**

"When the ordeal was over, the poor Celestial's tail was cut off, the worst punishment, in a social point of view, that can be, as it is what happens in the case of men convicted as '**laliloons**' or robbers."  ★★★★★

# Lamma Island

/lama/ *n.*

**Source language:** Cantonese (南丫島).

**Definition:** an island located southwest of Hong Kong Island, with many expatriate residents.  ★★★★★

# Lan Kwai Fong

/lan kwaɪ fɔŋ/ *n.*

**Source language:** Cantonese (蘭桂坊).

**Definition:** an (expatriate) drinking enclave.

**Text example:**

"Like Hong Kong itself **Lan Kwai Fong** is an invention ... Now dozens of restaurants bars, night clubs and coffee houses occupy the area and have transformed it into something almost approaching a foreign country."  ★★★★★

# Lantau Island

/ˈlæntaʊ ˈaɪlənd/ *n.*

**Source language:** Cantonese (爛頭山 old name) (大嶼山 modern name).

**Definition:** the name of the largest island in the HK SAR.

**Text example:**

"**Lantau**, the biggest island in Hong Kong, has long been recognized for its conservation and recreation values."

# Lantern Festival

*n.*

**Definition:** the fifteenth day of the Chinese New Year.

**Text example:**

"The Spring **Lantern Festival**, which is also known as Chinese Valentine's Day, marks the end of Chinese New Year celebrations."

See: **Chinese Valentine's Day**.

# lap sap

/laːp səp/ *n.*

**Source language:** Cantonese (垃圾).

**Definition:** rubbish or litter.

**Text example:**

"The bay is known as **Lap Sap** Wan which locally means 'Rubbish Bay', the name being derived from the large amount of rubbish that covers the beach there."

See: **lap sap chung**, **lap sap yan**.

# lap sap chung

/laːp səp tʃʌŋ/ *n.*

**Source language:** Cantonese (垃圾蟲).

**Definition:** a litter bug.

**Text example:**

"**Lap Sap Chung**, ... is the mascot for the Clean Hong Kong programme ... The widely recognised **Lap Sap Chung** is considered the most suitable choice to portray a negative image of people who litter."

# lap-sap yan/lo/po

/laːp səp jan/ *n.*

**Source language:** Cantonese (垃圾 人／佬／婆).

**Definition:** a person whose primary means of employment is the collecting of trash for recycling.

**Text example:**

❶ "She was smiling like a **lap-sap yan** asking for a lai see. Ignored her. As usual, bundle of stuff in her arms, looked like laundry, trash, paper & plastic bags."

❷ "Sometimes I think I am like those '**lap sap lo**' having a good time of his life by digging through garbages and leftover of others."

❸ "Good point FOTH but he is up against all those '**Lap Sap Po's**' who forage for a living."

# leng mo

/leŋ məʊ/ *n.*

**Source language:** Cantonese (嘲模).

**Definition:** young female pseudo-models.

**Text example:**

"Many have questioned the photo diary, asking why the company promotes me in the same manner as the **leng mo** (young models) instead of pushing my music."

# leung

/laŋ/ *n.*

**Source language:** Cantonese (兩).

**Definition:** 1/16 catty or 1 tael.

**Text example:**

"Gold is sold by the tael which is exactly the same as a **leung**, and you will find many banks selling gold in Hong Kong: the tael price is displayed right ..."

See: **catty**.

**Note:** The more common spelling outside of Hong Kong is *liang*.

# li

/li:/ *n.*

**Source language:** Mandarin (里).

**Definition:** Chinese distance measure equivalent to half a kilometer.

**Text example:**

"From San-li Pa we mounted 343 metres through firs and pines, a distance of 10 **li** to San-koh Ya, where we put up at a mountain block-house kept by a family named Chang."

# li man fu

/li mʌn fu:/ *n.*

**Source language:** Cantonese (理民府).

**Definition:** a special magistrate or judge (archaic and obscure).

**Text example:**

"Even the title of my appointment—**Li Man Fu**—was centuries old, an archaic imperial title."

# linchi

/liŋ tʃi:/ *n.*

**Source language:** Mandarin (凌遲).

**Definition:** punishment by dismemberment (archaic).

**Text example:**

"We should see an even more delightful spectacle—that of the cutting off of the arms and legs, and, finally, the beheading of a man who had murdered his brother ... the punishment named '**linchi**', which is reserved for the most terrible of all crimes—that against the sacred family."

**Note:** This should not be confused with the ninth-century Chinese sage Linji Yixuan (臨濟義玄).

# ling chih (also lin zhi)

/liŋ tʃiː/ *n.*

**Source language:** Cantonese (靈芝).

**Definition:** the fungus *Ganoderma lucidum* is believed in China to confer longevity and used as a symbol of this on Chinese ceramic ware.

**Text example:**

"The Cross stands upon a lotus, Buddhist symbol of purity, at each side of which are Daoist symbols, the **ling-chih**, or fungus of longevity."

# Lion Rock

*n.*

**Definition:** a 495-meter high rocky hill north of Kowloon Tong. When viewed from certain angles, it is similar to the shape of a crouching lion.

# little brother

*idiomatic expression.*

**Definition:** penis.

**Text example:**

"I used a fluorescent condom; it will be easier to look for his **little brother**."

# localization

*n.*

**Definition:** a switch in the ethnicity of a position of power.

**Text example:**

"The first local Administrative officer was not appointed until after the War, and they were not appointed in larger numbers until 1973, when Governor MacLehose's social and infrastructural programs necessitated greater **localization**. **Localization** of the top posts in the civil service proceeded however at a snail's pace."

# lolita

*adj.*

**Definition:** a style of clothing with emphasis on frilly decoration and femininity.

**Text example:**

"I enjoy doing stitches chokers of **Lolita** style because I have passionate in lace, ribbons, and jewelry making."

**Note:** Originally from Japan, where the term "Lolita fashion" was first coined.

# lo mei

/ləʊ meɪ/ *n.*

**Source language:** Cantonese (鹵味).

**Definition:** a style of meat stewed in a seasoned sauce.

**Text example:**

"Siu-mei and **lo-mei** are specially processed meat, poultry and offal products in Chinese cuisines. **Lo-mei** are braised and soaked in large volume of seasoning sauce for a period of time for flavour enrichment."

See: **siu mei**.

# lo mein

/ləʊ miːn/ *n.*

**Source language:** Cantonese (撈麵).

**Definition:** a variety of boiled wheat noodles, usually topped/mixed with sauce, e.g., oyster sauce, soy sauce, etc.

**Text example:**

"Barbecued meat buns, fishballs dripping with curry and stir-fried noodles, or **lo mein**, are all popular foods in Hong Kong."

# Lover's Day

*n.*

See: **Chinese Valentine's Day**.

# lucky money

*idiomatic expression.*

**Definition:** see **lai see**.

**Text example:**

"Shenzhen resident Huang Xiaoli said her family had paid extra '**lucky money**' to the doctor who operated on her grandmother last year."

Macanese
mace
MacLehose Trail
mafoo
mafu
mah-jong
mah-mah
maid
mai dan
Mainland
Mainlander
mamasan
mein
Mid-Autumn Festival
Mid-Levels
mil
Ming Dynasty egg
ming pai
Miss
mm goi (saai)
mm sai
mo lay tau
Mong Kok

# M

Monkey God Festival
moutai
mui tsai
mushroom pavilion/hut

# Macanese

*adj., n.*

**Definition:** ➊ relating to the Macanese people and their culture; ➋ the people of Macau; ➌ the people of Macau who are of mixed Portuguese and Chinese heritage.

**Text example:**

➊ "**Macanese** food is spicy, a unique combination of Chinese, Indian, Malay and Portuguese cooking methods."

➋ "**Macanese** go to polls today to choose legislators."

➌ "The tiny portion of Macau's population known as **Macanese**—the descendants of intermarriage between Portuguese and Chinese—fear they will lose their cultural identity now that nearly 500 years of Portuguese influence in Macau is ending." ★★★★★

# mace

*n.*

**Source language:** Malay.

**Definition:** 1/160 catty.

See: **catty**. ★★★★☆

# MacLehose Trail

*n.*

**Definition:** a 100-km hiking trail that starts in Sai Kung ending at Tuen Mun. The trail was named after Governor Murray MacLehose, who established the Country Parks. The Oxfam Trailwalker competition is run on this trail. ★★★☆☆

# mafoo (1)

/ **mafu:** / *n.*

**Source language:** Cantonese (馬伕).

**Definition:** a stable boy.
**Text example:**

"At the core of the **mafoo** row are two difficult issues—
the division of stake money and what happens to a **mafoo**
when a horse changes stables. A **mafoo** gets a percentage
of the stake money his horse wins."

# mafu (also **mafoo**) (2)

/ˈmafu:/ *idiomatic expression.*
**Source language:** Cantonese (馬伕).
**Definition:** a person who arranges customers for
prostitution and acts as an escort for prostitutes, often a
young triad member.
**Text example:**

❶ "Under caution, the Appellant admitted that she was
a '**Mafu**,' who took the girls to vice establishments
upon receiving a telephone call. She earned $20 or $40
commission for each girl she took to the establishments."

❷ "The escorts of these prostitutes, the '**Mafoos**,' normally
receive $60 and the villa keepers would take $100 to $120
for each visit by a prostitute."

**Underlying conceptualizations:** SEX IS RIDING, THE
PERSON WHO ARRANGES SEX IS A STABLE BOY [TARGET
DOMAIN ➡ SEX] [SOURCE DOMAIN ➡ RIDING].

See: **mafoo** (1).

# mah-jong (also **mahjongg**)

/mɑːˈdʒɔŋ/ *n.*
**Source language:** Cantonese (麻雀).
**Definition:** a four-player tile-based gambling game
similar to poker.
**Text example:**

❶ "Similar to applying skills to playing **mah-jong**, investors
should always think carefully when deciding what and
when to buy."

M

❷ "When there are few visitors in the winter season there are local people playing **mahjongg** or chatting over glasses of beer in some of those shops." ★★★★☆

# mah-mah

/ma: ma:/ *n.*
**Source language:** Cantonese (嬤嬤).
**Definition:** paternal grandmother.
**Text example:**

"I've mentioned before about how K was confused on what to call me. He started out by calling me, 'mama,' but once he started to call his paternal grandmother '**mah-mah**,' he got a little confused." ★★☆☆☆

# maid

*n.*
**Definition:** female domestic helper.
**Text example:**

"Hiring a **maid** on a part-time basis is illegal if the **maid** has a contract with another family." ★★★★★

# mai dan

/maɪ da:n/ *fixed expression.*
**Source language:** Cantonese (埋單).
**Definition:** the request for the bill in a restaurant (usually spoken language).
**Text example:**

"She looked at her watch and summoned a waiter Chinese style, her palm downwards and all her fingers beckoning together. '**Mai dan**, m'goi,' she said." ★★☆☆☆

# Mainland

*n.*
**Definition:** the People's Republic of China.

**Text example:**

"About 250,000 Hong Kong residents now work on the **Mainland**, almost double the number in 1997."

★★★★★

# Mainlander

*n.*

**Definition:** a person from the People's Republic of China.

**Text example:**

"There was a sharp differentiation between **mainlanders** and Hongkongers in popular media and social discourses."

★★★★☆

# mamasan

/mamasan/ *n.*

**Source language:** Japanese.

**Definition:** a woman who manages prostitutes.

**Text example:**

"You rang a buzzer to summon hard-faced **mamasans** or sharp-faced Chinese kids with gang written all over them."

★★★☆☆

# mein

/miːn/ *n.*

**Source language:** Cantonese (麵).

**Definition:** noodles.

**Text example:**

"The same could be said for those few remaining hole-in-the-wall homemade wonton **mein** or dumpling shops."

★★★★★

# Mid-Autumn Festival

*n.*

**Definition:** statutory holiday the day after the fifteenth day of the eighth month of the Chinese lunar calendar.

**Text example:**

"No statistically significant seasonal variations in the

incidence of burn were found except the days around the **mid-autumn festival** when children showed a peak rise in burn injuries."

# Mid-Levels

*n.*

**Definition:** a primarily residential area on Hong Kong Island, usually occupied by well-off expatriates.

**Text example:**

"The Western **Mid-Levels** is primarily a residential area located halfway between Central's business district and Victoria Peak. Many of the residents in the Western Midlevels are expatriates and people who work in Central. The Western **Mid-Levels** is considered a very prestigious area to live in."

# mil

/ **mil** / *n.*

**Source language:** Latin.

**Definition:** one-thousandth of a Hong Kong dollar (archaic).

**Text example:**

"With the denominations of coins ranging from one dollar down to one **mil**, which is a thousandth of a dollar, one **mil** would be roughly sufficient to buy a bowl of congee and a deep-fried dough. However, nowadays the one **mil** coin has become a highly treasured collectible."

# Ming Dynasty egg

*fixed expression.*

See: **century egg**.

# ming pai

/miŋ paɪ/ *n.*

**Source language:** Cantonese (名牌).

**Definition:** commercial brand names of high status.

**Text example:**

"As against the well-defined set of **ming pai** or famous brands that the nouveaux riches gravitate to, the nouveaux chic use a wider gamut of brands."

# Miss

*n.*

**Definition:** a title used instead of "Ms." by any adult woman married or not.

**Text example:**

"**Miss** Chan was born in Hong Kong in 1959 and is married with 2 children."

# mm goi (saai)

/m gɔɪ (saɪ)/ *fixed expression.*

**Source language:** Cantonese (唔該).

**Definition:** an expression equivalent to "thank you," but used only for service and not for a gift or a compliment (usually spoken language).

**Text example:**

"Thank you all—**mm-goi saai**!"

See: **do-jeh**.

# mm sai

/m saɪ/ *fixed expression.*

**Source language:** Cantonese (唔使).

**Definition:** don't mention it (in response to a "thank-you" for a service performed).

**Text example:**

"'Mm goi' (Thanks.) '**Mm sai**' (Don't mention it.)."

# mo lay tau

/məʊ leɪ taʊ/ *n.*

**Source language:** Cantonese (無厘頭).

**Definition:** nonsensical-style comedy, using vulgar Cantonese slang.

**Text example:**

> "For Li, **mo-lay-tau** ('nonsense slapsticks') is only the symptom of a desperate condition, not in itself a positive or creative response to any situation."

# Mong Kok

/mɔŋ kɔk/ /mɔŋ gɔk/ *n.*

**Source language:** Cantonese (旺角).

**Definition:** a crowded market and residential neighborhood in northern Yau Tsim Mong District.

# Monkey God Festival

*n.*

**Definition:** a non-statutory holiday on the sixteenth day of the eighth lunar month, during which devout followers will re-enact the traditional trials of the mischievous and playful god.

**Text example:**

> "Hot on the heels of the Mid-Autumn Festival is the festival celebrating the birthday of the most mischievous and resilient god in the Chinese pantheon—the Monkey God."

M

# moutai

/maʊ tɔi/ /maʊ daɪ/ *n.*

**Source language:** Mandarin, Cantonese (茅台酒).

**Definition:** alcoholic beverage of high status distilled from fermented sorghum in mountain water.

**Text example:**

"The drink—a 53 percent proof tipple made of mountain water, sorghum and grain—is steeped in communist lore. Though it traces its origins back two millennia, **Moutai** has been the drink of choice for generations of Communist leaders."

# mui tsai

/muːiːtsaɪ/ *n.*

**Source language:** Cantonese (妹仔).

**Definition:** ❶ an adopted female child servant, literally "little sister" (archaic); ❷ forced child labor (archaic).

**Text example:**

❶ "The '**mui tsai**,' literally meaning 'little sister,' were daughters who had been 'sold' by families in financial difficulties who urgently needed to raise funds."

❷ "The doctors said it was the first case in decades of **mui tsai**, the now-banned act of selling children into bonded labor, a practice widespread in the mainland, Hong Kong and Singapore right up to World War II."

# mushroom pavilion/hut

*fixed expression.*

**Definition:** open-air, mushroom-shaped, restaurant buildings typically built on public housing estates.

**Text example:**

❶ "The Link, which manages most public housing shopping centres in Hong Kong, plans to contribute 70 million for the renovation of 58 '**Mushroom Pavilions**' (open-air Dai Pai Dong) in its 26 public housing estates."

❷ "Finally, another tasty shop found in our increasingly rare **mushroom huts** is Shing Tai Noodles in Lok Wah Estate in Ngau Tau Kok."

See: **dai pai dong**.

**mushroom pavilion** (photo by P. J. Cummings)

M

# N

National Day
New Kowloon
New Territories
ni hao
Noonday Gun
North District
nullah

# National Day

*n.*

**Definition:** statutory holiday on October 1, celebrated across China.

**Text example:**

"There has been a fierce debate since May 1996 about whether or not the Church should celebrate China's **National Day**." ★★★★★

# New Kowloon

*n.*

**Source language:** Cantonese (新九龍).

**Definition:** an area of the city of Kowloon, bounded in the south by Boundary Street.

**Text example:**

"In 1965, 32 per cent of all jobs were located on Hong Kong island, 48 per cent in Kowloon and **New Kowloon**, and only 20 per cent in the New Territories." ★★★★★

# New Territories

*n.*

**Definition:** the part of Hong Kong leased from China for 99 years, north of Boundary Street and south of the border between Hong Kong and the Mainland, as well as the outlying islands.

**Text example:**

"**New Territories**, abbreviated to NT or N.T., is a region in Hong Kong excluding Hong Kong Island, Kowloon and Stonecutters Island." ★★★★★

# ni hao

/niː haʊ/ *fixed expression.*
**Source language:** Mandarin (你好).
**Definition:** hello.
**Text example:**

"**Ni Hao** Dear Mr. Sit, Thank you for the inspiring books."

**Note:** During the morning time, *jo san* is used, while Mainlanders and Taiwanese use *ni hao* throughout the day. ★★★★☆

# Noonday Gun

*fixed expression.*
**Definition:** a naval gun fired at noon by the company Jardines.
**Text example:**

"At 12:00 noon every day, a one-shot salvo is fired at the side of the sea in Causeway Bay. This is the **Noonday Gun**, fired by Jardine Matheson Group, one of the oldest British hongs in Hong Kong, for more than 140 years."

★★★★☆

# North District

*n.*
**Definition:** a district in the northeastern New Territories adjacent to the Mainland border and the Mainland city of Shenzhen, containing the towns of Fan Ling and Sheung Shui. ★★★★★

N

# nullah

/nʌla/ *n.*

**Source language:** Indian English.

**Definition:** a small river.

**Text example:**

> "Four other **nullahs** will be decked by 2011 as time is needed to resolve more complicated engineering and land constraints."

**Note:** This term is usually used in HKE for place names such as Nullah Road. The use of *nullah* in the sense of a "small river" is becoming archaic in HKE.

**nullah** in Causeway Bay, c. 1920s
(Source: Public domain, Wikimedia Commons)

# O

OK
Old China Hand
one big pot wages
one country two systems
overtime

# OK

*n.*

**Source language:** Japanese.

**Definition:** karaoke.

**Text example:**

> "'Karaoke' (**OK**) means an activity in which a person, by himself or, together with one or more than one other person, chants, intones, sings or vocalizes in association with or in company with any music or other sound, or any visual image or other information ..."

**Note:** This term is not related to the English expression "O.K."

# Old China Hand

*idiomatic expression.*

**Definition:** an expatriate with many years of experience in Hong Kong and/or China.

**Text example:**

> "Within the Foreign office, the China experts, the **Old China Hands**, are a select breed."

# one big pot wages

*idiomatic expression.*

**Definition:** egalitarian wages.

**Text example:**

> "There has been a corrosion of the so-called 'iron rice bowl' (lifetime employment), '**one big pot**' (egalitarian) **wages** have been eroded, and there has been increasing exploitation not just in foreign-invested enterprises, but also in the transforming state-owned enterprises and non-traditional sectors of work."

**Underlying conceptualizations:** SALARY IS FOOD, EQUAL PAY IS EATING FROM THE SAME FOOD CONTAINER.

[TARGET DOMAIN ➜ SALARY] [SOURCE DOMAINS ➜ FOOD, FOOD CONTAINER].

See: **golden rice bowl**, **iron rice bowl**.

# one country two systems

*fixed expression.*

**Definition:** a political concept by Deng Xiaoping, a former leader of China, for reunification with Hong Kong, Macau and Taiwan. Under this concept the returning territories can have their own capitalist economic and political systems, while Mainland China uses the socialist system.

**Text example:**

"One would expect there to be free mobility of labour within a country, but this is not the case under '**one country, two systems**.'"

# overtime

*n.*

**Definition:** hours worked beyond the normally agreed-on time, without pay.

**Text example:**

"Employees in Hong Kong work very long hours: The average working week in Hong Kong is 55 hours. 80% of people regularly work unpaid **overtime**. 75% of people work late into the evenings."

paddy
pai lau
pajamas (pyjamas)
pak choi
pak pai
palm civet
panel teacher
pang uk
pantyhose tea/coffee
paper money
Parsi
passport holder
passport prison
passport widow
pearl milk tea
Pearl of the Orient/East
pei daan
penang lawyer
picul
poon choi
po-po
pork chop
praya
princeling
pro-China
Pu-er

# P

Punti
Putonghua

# paddy

/ˈpadiː/ *n.*

**Source language:** Malay.

**Definition:** unpolished rice that has not had the outer husk removed.

**Text example:**

"Mr. Tang is a mixed farmer and **paddy** is his principal crop, but the main part of the rice plays in the economy of this family is to feed them and the labourers." ★★★★☆

# pai lau

/paɪ ləʊ/ *n.*

**Source language:** Cantonese (牌樓).

**Definition:** a decorative archway not normally attached to a building, often symmetrical with three openings and four pillars.

**Text example:**

"At the entrance gateway of the landscaped piazza, there is a new **Pai Lau** in Qing Dynasty Northern style matching with the architectural style of Po Lin Monastery." ★★☆☆☆

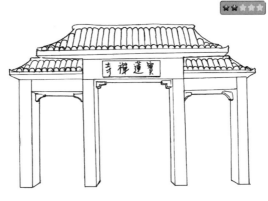

**pai lau** (drawing by Adrian Cennydd Petyt)

# pajamas (also pyjamas)

*n.*

**Source language:** Indian English.

**Definition:** casual clothing of a particular style, which can be worn in public (a practice becoming less common).

**Text example:**

❶ "The Jumbo was also quintessential Hong Kong in staggering cost of a meal ... ; unfathomably, the place still filled up in the afternoons with tables of grannies and their adolescent wards in the modified **pajamas** that are the everyday garb of the Cantonese working class."

❷ "In this city of contrasts, executives in pin-stripes suits rub shoulders with elderly man in **pyjamas** taking their songbirds for a walk along city streets." ★★★★★

# pak choi (also pak choy)

/bək tʃɔɪ/ /pək tʃɔɪ/ *n.*

See: **bok choy**.

# pak pai

/bək paɪ/ *n.*

**Source language:** Cantonese (白牌).

**Definition:** an unregistered and illegal taxi (archaic).

**Text example:**

"Is it true that Government intends to legalize **Pak Pai** cars which have been running illegally as taxis in the Colony?" ★★☆☆☆

# palm civet

*n.*

**Definition:** see **civet cat**.

**Text example:**

"Isolation of the SARS associated coronavirus (SARS-

CoV) from palm civet (*Paguma larvata*) and phylogenetic analysis suggested that **palm civet** is an intermediate host, which transmitted the disease to human." ★★★☆☆

# panel teacher

*n.*

**Definition:** a school department head.

**Text example:**

"She did not know when he was promoted from the position of a teacher to that of **panel teacher** and later, headmaster." ★★☆☆☆

# pang uk

/paːŋ ək/ *n.*

**Source language:** Cantonese (棚屋).

**Definition:** a type of house built on stilts above water or small beaches.

**Text example:**

"Houses at Tai O are built on stilts and many have tin walls (below). The local name for this style is **pang uk**, which literally means 'stilted house.'"

**Note:** Typical of old buildings in Tai O. ☆☆☆☆☆

# pantyhose tea/coffee

*idiomatic expression.*

**Definition:** a Hong Kong method of beverage preparation using a net-like filter that looks like a panty hose, but is specifically made for filtering tea/coffee.

**Text example:**

 ❶ "**Pantyhose tea** is regarded as the smoothest, silkiest version of Hong Kong's favorite drink—creamy milk tea, which is made with evaporated milk and a heavy dose of tea leaves. It's nothing like watered-down English tea."

❷ "A similar drink is '**Pantyhose coffee**', made with coffee instead of tea."

See: **silk-stocking tea**.

**pantyhose coffee** (photo by P. J. Cummings)

# paper money
*n.*
See: **spirit money**.

# Parsi (also **Parsee**)
/ˈpaːrsiː/ *n., adj.*
**Source language:** Old Persian.
**Definition:** a member of an Indian ethnic minority who are followers of the Persian bronze-age Prophet Zarathushtra (Zoroaster).
**Text example:**

❶ "In 1889, apart from the 790 Chinese and Eurasians, 131 boys of various creeds and nationalities (including English, Hebrews, Germans, Japanese, Moslems, Portuguese, one Hindu and a **Parsee**) were registered in the Central School."

❷ "Sir Hormusjee N. Mody (1838–1911) Major donor towards the founding of The University of Hong Kong, a distinguished **Parsi** Businessman, renowned

P

philanthropist & benefactor of Hong Kong for over fifty years."

**Note:** Happy Valley, Hong Kong Island, has a "Parsee Cemetery."

# passport holder

*fixed expression.*

**Definition:** a person who holds a passport, but does not necessarily feel any loyalty as a citizen; used to describe people holding passports of convenience.

**Text example:**

"Greg So Kam-leung, former vice-chairman of the Democratic Alliance for the Betterment and Progress of Hong Kong, a former professionally qualified lawyer in Canada and former Canadian **passport holder**, has just started his new job as undersecretary of the Commerce and Economic Development Bureau."

# passport prison

*idiomatic expression.*

**Definition:** a country in which you are living solely for the purpose of obtaining a passport.

**Text example:**

"Emigration numbers dropped off sharply after 1997. By then, everyone who wanted to and was able to leave, had left. Some had even begun to trickle back after serving their requisite years overseas in '**passport prison**.'"

# passport widow

*idiomatic expression.*

**Definition:** a wife living apart from her husband while she lives overseas in order to obtain a passport.

**Text example:**

"These my friends, Chen-Tai, Chiu-Tai and Law-Tai. All '**passport widows**' like me."

# pearl milk tea

*n.*

See: **bubble tea**.

# Pearl of the Orient/East

*idiomatic expression.*

**Definition:** a nickname for Hong Kong (although this expression is also used for other places).

**Text example:**

❶ "HONG KONG—THE **PEARL OF THE ORIENT** AND ITS LUSTER Hong Kong captures the world's imagination like no other place on the face of earth."

❷ A Hong Kong which is not able to pull itself together to confront intensifying global competition will no longer be the shining **Pearl of the East**, but will instead become the liability of China and signify the inoperativeness of Beijing's policy of 'one country, two systems.'"

# pei daan

/peɪ daːn/ *n.*

**Source language:** Mandarin (皮蛋).

See: **century egg**.

# penang lawyer

/pəˈnæŋ ˈlɔːjə/ *n.*

**Source language:** Malay.

**Definition:** a walking stick made from the stem of *Licuala acutifida* (archaic).

**Text example:**

"For instance under the word lawyer, the well-known **'Penang lawyer'** (we have always been told) is simply a native term, and should be spelt loyah, or in some such wise."

**P**

**Note:** There is no relationship between Penang lawyer and the meaning of "lawyer." The *penang lawyer* was a hard, but occasionally brittle walking-stick exported from Penang and Singapore. The name suggests such sticks may have helped resolve disputes through violence. However, the name derives from the *pinang lāyor* (fire-dried areca). The similarity of *lāyor* to "lawyer" is coincidental.

# picul

/pikəl/ *n.*
**Source language:** Malay.
**Definition:** 100 catties.
**Text example:**

"It discovered that pak choi (white cabbage) was sold by the New Territories farmer at $3.50 per **picul**, by the vegetable loan or wholesaler at $12 per **picul**, and by the market stall-holder at $14 in Kowloon and $18 per **picul** in Hong Kong."

See: **catty**.

# poon choi

/puːn tʃɔɪ/ *n.*
**Source language:** Hakka (盆菜).
**Definition:** a traditional food served in a large basin, with many layers of different meats, seafood, and vegetables.
**Text example:**

"He also said there were more cases of food poisoning at the start of the Year of the Dog, mostly due to the popularity of **poon choi**, the seafood-charged 'big bowl feast' traditionally served during the Lunar New Year."

# po-po (also **pohpo**, **pohpoh**)

/pɔ pɔ/ *n.*

**Source language:** Cantonese (婆婆).

**Definition:** maternal grandmother.

**Text example:**

❶ "Bye, Grandmother. I'm so happy to know my **po-po**."

❷ "That was probably why she'd overlooked her cousin, because **pohpo** died the year before she left for Canada."

❸ "His **PohPoh** and KongKong are getting older so I'd really like to meet them sometime." ⭐⭐⭐⭐

# pork chop

*idiomatic expression.*

**Definition:** a fat and ugly woman (derogatory).

**Text example:**

"... called her a '**pork chop**' and pointed and leered at her breasts." ⭐⭐

# praya

/praɪjə/ *n.*

**Source language:** Portuguese.

**Definition:** waterfront where ships are likely to dock (archaic).

**Text example:**

"The reclamation was carried out between 1890 and 1904 to extend the **praya** northwards to the present Connaught Road. The original **praya** was then renamed Des Voeux road to commemorate the Governor Sir William Des Voeux."

**Note:** Now usually used in HK only as a place name. Outside of HKE the spelling *praia* is more common.

 ⭐⭐⭐⭐⭐

P

# princeling

*idiomatic expression.*

**Definition:** a child or other relative of a high-ranking Chinese Communist official, who gains special privileges.

**Text example:**

"And, just as important, Zhu is not a '**princeling**,' an offspring of a top Chinese cadre who rose to power and influence in part because of family ties. Vice Premier Zhu is said to have banned **princelings** from Hong Kong."

# pro-China

*adj.*

**Definition:** supporting the national government of the People's Republic of China.

**Text example:**

"Its leader, Tsang Yok-shing, proclaimed his party as '**pro-China**,' but even more pro-Hong Kong,' complaining that the public did not appreciate this point."

**Note:** In HKE, *pro-China* is the opposite of pro-democracy, not the opposite of unpatriotic.

# Pu-er

/pu: ər/ *n.*

**Source language:** Mandarin (普洱) (Pu'er county, Yunnan, China).

**Definition:** a popular type of tea.

**Text example:**

"This paper-wrapped tea is made from high-quality **Pu-er**, steamed and compressed to mushroom shape of about 2.4 cm in diameter. The history of this tea can be traced back to Ming Dynasty (AD 1368–1644)."

# Punti

/pʌnti:/ /buːndeɪ/ *n.*

**Source language:** Cantonese (本地).

**Definition:** ❶ Cantonese; ❷ of local origin.

**Text example:**

❶ "It is interesting to note the early censuses used language as the means of distinguishing between Hakka and **Punti** (Hong Kong Government 1911)."

❷ "In Hong Kong **Punti** are legally classified as those who resided in the New Territories before 1898; thus, members of a number of older Hakka lineages are classified as **Punti**." ★★★★☆

# Putonghua

/puːtɔːŋhwa:/ *n.*

**Source language:** Mandarin (普通話).

**Definition:** the official national language of China, in the process of being established since the Communist came to power (literally "common speech"), also known as Mandarin.

**Text example:**

"In fact, many of Hong Kong Chinese could not speak Chinese (mandarin, **putonghua**)." ★★★★★

# pyjamas

*n.*

See: **pajamas**.

# Q

**qigong**

# qigong

/tʃiːgɔŋ/ *n.*

**Source language:** Mandarin (氣功).

**Definition:** a set of breathing and movement exercises.

**Text example:**

"First you indulge in a **Qigong** session (the ancient Chinese art of energy work, $800) followed by a spot of Past Life Therapy ($3,000), in which your therapist will take you back to a previous life and help you complete any unfinished business."

red capitalist
red chip
red packet/pocket (money)
red pole (fighter)
Renminbi
reprovisioning
rice Christian
rickshaw
right of abode
rubbish

# R

# red capitalist

*idiomatic expression.*

**Definition:** a Mainland business person who uses a socialist self-description.

**Text example:**

> "Indeed, one reason for the sending of so-called '**red capitalist**' Wang Guangying to Hong Kong was—so Wang himself openly hinted—because of dissatisfaction in the Chinese politburo with China Resources."

★★☆☆☆

# red chip

*idiomatic expression.*

**Definition:** (stocks of) companies that are based in the Mainland or have significant Mainland business connections.

**Text example:**

> "Many **red chips** are considering a return to the domestic equity markets to raise capital or as a way of supporting Beijing's policy to enhance the quality of bourses—but only few of them can issue yuan-denominated A shares, given the relatively high requirements."

★★★★☆

# red packet/pocket (money)

*fixed expression.*

**Definition:** see **lai see**.

**Text example:**

❶ "Students are given some **red packets** (only one **red packet** contains a 10-dollar bank note)."

❷ "Anybody is [*sic*] still single loves the Chinese New Year because they are entitled to receive the **red pocket money** from the married people."

★★★★☆

R

# red pole (fighter)

*idiomatic expression.*

**Definition:** a senior member of a triad society.

**Text example:**

"Once a boxer, he went by the nickname 'Thai Lung' and became a '**red pole**' for the society. A **red pole** is a senior member who usually plays an enforcing role."

See: **triad**.

# Renminbi

/renminbi:/ *n.*

**Source language:** Mandarin (人民幣).

**Definition:** Mainland currency, equivalent to the yuan.

**Text example:**

"The official currency of the People's Republic of China (PRC) is **Renminbi** (meaning in Chinese: 'people's currency')."

See: **jiao**, **yuan**, **fen**.

# reprovisioning

*n.*

**Definition:** to provide a resource again after it has been removed or consumed.

**Text example:**

"The Government spokesman said, 'We would welcome public comments on the in-situ **reprovisioning** and operation of the STWTW and related facilities through PPP.'"

**Note:** This word and its meaning is not specific to HKE, but in HKE, usage seems to be restricted to the domain of publications or statements from the HK government, where this word occurs more frequently.

R

# rice Christian

*idiomatic expression.*

**Definition:** a convert to Christianity for material gain (possibly archaic).

**Text example:**

"Chinese friends and colleagues asked me about Christianity and were disappointed that they could not attend my church, not realising that it was forbidden. When I declared Good Friday a non-working day, one Chinese colleague wanted to 'convert' on the spot—a modern-day example of a '**rice Christian**'!"

# rickshaw

/ˈrikʃɔː/ *n.*

**Source language:** Japanese.

**Definition:** a human-powered buggy for city travel, usually providing a taxi service.

**Text example:**

"Any owner of a **rickshaw** who wishes to have the **rickshaw** licensed shall—(a) deliver to the Commissioner an application therefore in a form specified by the Commissioner which shall be accompanied by his identity document."

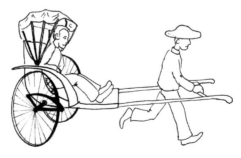

**rickshaw** (drawing by Adrian Cennydd Petyt)

R

146

# right of abode

*legal term.*

**Definition:** legal authorization to reside in Hong Kong.

**Text example:**

"A new survey casts serious doubt on the reliability of the Government's claim that 1.603 million 'additional' Mainlanders are eligible for **right of abode** on the basis of the Court of Final Appeal's judgments of 29 January 1999."

★★★★★

# rubbish

*v.*

**Definition:** to discard worthless material in an inappropriate place, usually on the ground.

**Text example:**

"He urged members of the public to sustain their keep clean efforts and to let the message of the campaign slogan 'There is never any excuse to **rubbish** your home' stride across the new Millennium."

★★★☆☆

R

Sai Kung
salt-baked chicken
samfoo
sampan
sampan congee
samshu
sandwich class
sars
school brother/sister
second kitchen
sedan chair
Sevens, Hong Kong
Seven Sisters Festival
Sham Shui Po District
shan
Shanghai foot
Shanghailanders
Shanghainese
shao mai
Sha Tin
Shenzhen
Sheung Shui
Shing Mun River
shoe of gold
shoeshine boy
short-time hotel
shroff
shroffing
shu mai
-side
sifu
silk-stocking milk tea
si mutt lai cha
sitting-out area
siu mai
siu mei
small chow
smelly (stinky) tofu

snakehead
SoHo
Southern District
spiders (spidermen)
spirit money
splittist
staffs
Stonecutter's Island
Suzie Wong
swallow nest
sycee

S

# Sai Kung

/saɪ kuŋ/ *n.*

**Source language:** Cantonese (西貢).

**Definition:** a town, park and district in the southeastern New Territories. ⭐⭐⭐⭐⭐

# salt-baked chicken

*n.*

**Definition:** a chicken dish baked inside a heap of hot salt, simply cooked in brine or covered with a salty mixture before steaming it or baking it in an oven.

**Text example:**

"The menu includes such signature Hakka dishes as the delicious **salt-baked chicken**, handmade fish balls and braised meats and tofu, as well as a twist on Shanghainese drunken chicken, done here with a sweet, delicate rose flavor." ⭐⭐⭐⭐⭐

# samfoo (also samfu)

/samfu:/ *n.*

**Source language:** Cantonese (衫褲).

**Definition:** a style of clothing consisting of a high-necked jacket and loose pants, no longer common.

**Text example:**

❶ "Stock changes regularly at stalls likes these, so come back in summer for rayon blouses and delicately patterned, lightweight **samfoo** (pyjama suit) outfits."

❷ "In the 70's my friends had middle-aged amahs with green jade earrings and black **samfu**." ⭐⭐☆☆☆

# sampan

/sa:mpən/ *n.*

**Source language:** Cantonese (舢舨).

**Definition:** a small, flat-bottomed boat.

**Text example:**

"On 29 April 2004 at about 1330, an open **sampan** fitted with outboard engine was reported to have sunk near the coast of Tai Long Wan in Sai Kung."

**Note:** From the Cantonese number three, *sam*, and boards, *pan*, which was probably a reference to the original size of the boat.

**sampan** (drawing by Adrian Cennydd Petyt)

# sampan congee

*n.*

**Definition:** a popular Hong Kong variety of congee with a variety of ingredients often including seafood, pork, and tofu.

**Text example:**

"A bowl of **sampan congee** with one fried bread stick contains 49 grams of fat, which is more than half of the amount needed by a normal person, and a rather high level of saturated fat and cholesterol."

See: **boat congee**, **congee**.

# samshu (also samsu, samshoo)

/saːmʃuː/ *n.*

**Source language:** Chinese Pidgin English.

**Definition:** an alcoholic beverage made from rice.

**Text example:**

❶ "They consented, and themselves procured some **samshu**. All apparently drank from the same brew, but the host was the only one affected."

❷ "The difficulty is that the alternative to toddy is **samsu**, a drink of such peculiar potency that the Tamil feels it is well worth the extra cost."

❸ "Salted meat and fish is soaked in sweet **samshoo** spiced with Red Cardamom Seeds." ★☆☆☆☆

# sandwich class

*idiomatic expression.*

**Definition:** those Hong Kong people "sandwiched" between the untaxed poor, who receive housing benefits, and the under-taxed rich; a synonym for "middle class."

**Text example:**

"Attention was focused on the plight of the so-called **sandwich class**." ★★★★☆

# sars

/saːz/ *n.*

**Definition:** derived from the acronym for severe acute respiratory syndrome, a disease caused by the SARS-CoV coronavirus.

**Text example:**

"I remember last year at the end of the **Sars** crisis in Hong Kong and China ..."

**Note:** The spelling and the corresponding pronunciation indicates that the acronym "SARS" is used as a regular word. ★★★★★

# school brother/sister

*n.*

**Definition:** a person from the same school.

**Text example:**

❶ "Making its DVD debut, *The Prisoner* is actually ten years old, and marks another pairing of Jackie with his old opera **school brother**, and a martial arts star and director in his own right, Sammo Hung."

❷ "My **school sister** who likes my friend called me to ask how to get the number of my friend."

**Underlying conceptualization:** A FELLOW MEMBER OF A SOCIAL GROUP ONE BELONGS TO IS A SIBLING [TARGET DOMAIN ➡ FELLOW MEMBER OF A SOCIAL GROUP] [SOURCE DOMAIN ➡ FAMILY].

See: **big brother**.

# second kitchen

*idiomatic expression.*

**Definition:** ❶ the provisional legislature set up in Shenzhen prior to the 1997 handover of Hong Kong; ❷ the practice of a married son and his wife living with his parents.

**Text example:**

❶ "The alternative course was to put in place the '**second kitchen**'—a process whereby the 150 members of the Preparatory Committee would prepare to appoint a Chief Executive and a provisional legislature in 1996."

❷ "Establishing a '**second kitchen**' relates to the Chinese custom of a married son setting up a **second kitchen** in his father's household."

# sedan chair

*n.*

**Definition:** ❶ a chair used to carry a bride to her new husband's house; ❷ formerly a conveyance for lazy expatriates.

**Text example:**

❶ "Come the wedding day the groom's family would send a

bridal **sedan-chair** to take her from her parents' village to his home."

❷ "Before the Peak Tram, however, the only way for Peak residents to commute between their prestigious address at 1,800 feet and bustling Central where most business and government activities took place was by **sedan chairs** and rickshaws." ★★★★☆

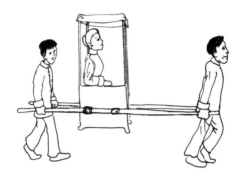

**sedan chair** (drawing by Adrian Cennydd Petyt)

# Sevens, Hong Kong

*n.*

**Definition:** an international rugby competition held in Hong Kong.

**Text example:**

"Since its establishment in 1976, certain features of the **Hong Kong Sevens** have become traditional—the spectators' comical hats and costumes, logo-emblazoned T-shirts, and painted faces; the Mexican Waves; ... the carnival atmosphere; and above all the rapturous roars when a favourite team scores a try." ★★★★☆

# Seven Sisters Festival

*n.*

**Definition:** a non-statutory holiday for girls and young

lovers on the seventh day of the seventh month of the lunar calendar.

**Text example:**

"The **Seven Sisters Festival** was initiated by unmarried girls for an audience of families, neighbors, and fellow villagers. According to informants, Seven Sisters 'associations' consisted of from ten to more than twenty unmarried girls from one or more girls' houses."

# Sham Shui Po District

/ʃəm ʃɔɪ pəʊ 'dɪstrɪkt/ *n.*

**Source language:** Cantonese (深水埗).

**Definition:** a district in part of western Kowloon peninsula.

# shan

/ʃan/ *n.*

**Source language:** Cantonese (山).

**Definition:** hill.

**Text example:**

"Tai Ping **Shan** Street, which runs above and parallel to Hollywood Road and the streets around it, conveys the impression of an entirely different time and place by comparison with both the modern shopping malls of Central and the fast-food establishments and electronic goods shops below in Sheung Wan."

**Note:** Usually only used for place names in HKE.

# Shanghai foot

*idiomatic expression.*

**Text example:**

"Shanghailanders aptly named this malady 'Hong Kong Foot' while residents of Hong Kong referred to it as **'Shanghai Foot.'**"

**See: Hong Kong foot**.

# Shanghailanders

*n.*

**Definition:** people from Shanghai.

**Text example:**

"It is perhaps a mark of the **Shanghailanders'** impact on Hong Kong that, despite their relatively late arrival, they give the impression that they have always been there."

★★★☆☆

# Shanghainese

*adj.*

**Definition:** of Shanghai, its people, language or food.

**Text example:**

"The importance of **Shanghainese** industrialists in the local economy is legendary."

★★★★★

# shao mai

*n.*

See: **siu mai**.

# Sha Tin

/ ʃa tɪn/ *n.*

**Source language:** Cantonese (沙田).

**Definition:** a district in the middle of Hong Kong containing a town of the same name built along the Shing Mun River Channel.

★★★★★

# Shenzhen

/ ʃenzen/ *n.*

**Source language:** Cantonese (深圳).

**Definition:** a Mainland city bordering on the north of Hong Kong.

★★★★★

S

# Sheung Shui

/ʃʌŋ ʃɔɪ/ *n.*

**Source language:** Cantonese (上水).

**Definition:** a growing market town in the North District; originally a walled village. ★★★★★

# Shing Mun River

/ʃiŋ mun 'rivə/ *n.*

**Source language:** Cantonese (城門河).

**Definition:** an artificial river flowing through Sha Tin into Tolo Harbour. ★★★★★

# shoe of gold

*idiomatic expression.*

**Definition:** a style of ingot for precious metals found in China (archaic).

**Text example:**

"Two of the images seem to be local Earth Gods. They have a '**shoe**' **of gold** in their left hand, long white beards, white eyebrows and white hair under a green." ★★★★★

# shoeshine boy (also shoe-shiner)

*idiomatic expression.*

**Definition:** a derogatory term for a sycophant, similar in use to the common English term "bootlicker."

**Text example:**

❶ "And now??? A **shoeshine boy** of the Communist Party!!!"

❷ "Now, for the sake of the nation, the loyalists will have to hold their tongues or actually perform the pro-Beijing zombie **shoe-shiner** act and mouth the official reality." ★★★★★

**S**

# short-time hotel

*fixed expression.*

**Definition:** a hotel that rents rooms by the hour, presumably for acts of prostitution.

**Text example:**

"I made arrangements and mamasan told me there was a '**short-time**' hotel that would meet our needs. The services were sold under the guise of massage."

**Note:** The use of a *short-time hotel* does suggest temporary sexual relationships but this is not its exclusive purpose. In HK, especially in the past, it has not been uncommon for six adults to share a one-room flat or for newly married poor couples to share a small flat with parents. A short-time hotel can be a place for legitimately married couples to go for sexual relations, when privacy is not available at home. ★★★★☆

# shroff

/ʃrɔf/ *n.*

**Source language:** Indian English.

**Definition:** a cashier, money changer or banker.

**Text example:**

"Tenants can pay their rents at any of the HA's **shroff** offices during office hours simply by presenting the e-Payment Card." ★★★★★

**shroff** (photo by P. J. Cummings)

# shroffing

*v.*

**Definition:** performing the work of a shroff.

**Text example:**

"**Shroffing** hours for Monday to Friday: 8.30 am to 1 pm, 2 pm to 5 pm." ★★★★☆

# shu mai

*n.*

See: **siu mai**.

# -side

*suffix.*

**Source language:** Chinese Pidgin English.

**Definition:** Kowloon side or Hong Kong side of the harbor.

**Text example:**

"Hong Kong is divided into three distinct areas: Hong Kong Island (often referred to as 'Hong Kong-**side**', 'the island', 'HK island'), Kowloon ('Kowloon-**side**'), and the New Territories." ★★★★★

# sifu

/ˈsiːfuː/ *n.*

**Source language:** Cantonese (師傅).

**Definition:** master craftsman.

**Text example:**

"Many Hong Kong cheongsam tailors were 'Shanghai' tailors, having been apprenticed to a master tailor (**sifu**) from Shanghai." ★★★☆☆

S

# silk-stocking milk tea

*idiomatic expression.*

**Definition:** a Hong Kong method of beverage preparation using a net-like filter that looks like a silk-stocking, but is specifically made for filtering tea/coffee.

**Text example:**

"Traditionally, the tea is infused in a silk sock, giving it the Cantonese nickname of si mat lai cha—literally **'silk stocking tea.'**"

See: **pantyhose tea.**

# si mutt lai cha

/si: mʌt laɪ tʃa:/ *n.*

**Source language:** Cantonese (絲襪奶茶). *Si mutt* is Cantonese for "pantyhose."

See: **pantyhose tea/coffee, lai cha.**

# sitting-out area

*fixed expression.*

**Definition:** a small urban Hong Kong park.

**Text example:**

"There are some benches along the way and a **sitting-out area** that is nicely shaded right at the beginning."

# siu mai (also **shu mai, shaomai**)

/ʃu: maɪ/ *n.*

**Source language:** Cantonese (燒賣).

**Definition:** a type of dim sum, containing ground steamed pork and possibly other meat.

**Text example:**

❶ "Nancy readies her chopsticks for another stab at a **siu mai**, then asks, 'What is it we're going to do with this testimony if we get it?'"

❷ "I love the **shu mai**, har gou, and cheong fun. God now I'm hungry for all that stuff."

❸ "Within the package, some sauces like soy sauce, vinegar, and spicy sauce can be provided for serving the food such as **Shaomai**, Cheong Fun or else as to be more convenient for serving." ⭐⭐⭐☆☆

**siu mai** (photo by P. J. Cummings)

# siu mei

/suː meɪ/ *n.*

**Source language:** Cantonese (燒味).

**Definition:** a roasted marinated meat.

**Text example:**

"In accordance with the laws of Hong Kong, any person who intends to operate a **Siu Mei** and Lo Mei shop business at any premises in the territory must obtain a **Siu Mei** and Lo Mei shop licence issued by the Licensing Authority before commencement of such business."

See: **lo mei**.

**Note:** This is a very different food from what is designated by *siu mai*. ⭐⭐⭐⭐☆

S

# small chow

/smɔːl tʃaʊ/ *n.*

**Source language:** Chinese Pidgin English.

**Definition:** fingerfood, hors d'oeuvres, or snacks.

**Text example:**

> "The spread on the altar table beside the bar made ludicrous the Hong Kong term for hors d'oeuvres or snacks, which was small chow."

# smelly (stinky) tofu

*fixed expression.*

**Definition:** a fermented tofu, with a strong odor.

**Text example:**

> "Fish balls, pig's colon or **smelly tofu**?"

# snakehead

*idiomatic expression.*

**Definition:** ❶ a leader of a people-smuggling gang; ❷ The name for such a gang itself (term gaining international acceptance).

**Text example:**

> ❶ "'We are not jumping the queue because there was no queue to follow at all,' a Mrs Chan, who paid a **'snakehead'** to smuggle her eight-year-old son from Guangzhou to Hong Kong last December, said."

> ❷ "Many of the illegal immigrants pay the **Snakehead** organizations in Hong Kong and Fujian up to $35000 for the passage."

# SoHo

*n.*

**Definition:** "South of Hollywood Road"; a non-Asian commercial and social enclave on Hong Kong Island.

S

**Text example:**

"Central **SoHo** is full of foreign atmosphere and it is an ideal place to enjoy western music." ★★★★★

# Southern District

*n.*

**Definition:** a district in the southern part of Hong Kong Island, containing many country parks. ★★★★★

# spiders (also spidermen)

*n.*

**Definition:** bamboo scaffolding workers.

**Text example:**

❶ "Visitors are often amazed at the sight of bamboo scaffolding rising high up the sides of Hong Kong's skyscrapers, and the gravity-defying skills of local bamboo scaffolders, often called '**spiders**.'"

❷ "Look up to see the '**spidermen**' of the city erect giant webs of bamboo scaffolding." ★★☆☆☆

# spirit money (also paper money, hell money, hell bank notes)

*fixed expressions*, *n.*

**Definition:** fake money burned in a ritual offering to the dead.

**spirit money** (drawing by Adrian Cennydd Petyt)

**Text example:**

❶ "We passed a hillock and saw little mounds of earth which were graves. It was just a day after Ching Ming. Men and women were milling about the graves and ashes from **spirit money** drifted in the air-like butterflies."

❷ "An offering of oranges may be peeled and placed on the grave, together with **paper money**. Finally, crackers are let off."

❸ "The **Hell Money** I used to buy as a kid was always green, ... because it was made for American Chinese people ... But in Hong Kong and Singapore, there is no such drab restriction on the colour of money. There, as witness the lovely **Hell Bank Note** for 5000,000,000 dollars, **Hell Money** can be a real work of art."

**Underlying conceptualizations:** A SUPERNATURAL BEING IS A HUMAN BEING, A PAPER MODEL IS A REAL OBJECT IN THE SUPERNATURAL WORLD [TARGET DOMAINS ➡ SUPERNATURAL BEING, PAPER MODEL] [SOURCE DOMAINS ➡ HUMAN BEING, OBJECT IN THE SUPERNATURAL WORLD].

See: **hell**.

# splittist

*n., adj.*

**Definition:** a person who wants independence for territory claimed by Beijing.

**Text example:**

"A Hong Kong member of the Standing Committee of the National People's Congress, Tsang Hin-chi, urged the broadcaster to exercise 'self-control' and not to provide a channel for '**splittist** views' (those advocating independence for Taiwan)."

# staffs

*n.*

**Definition:** members of staff.

**Text example:**

> "The Hong Kong Institute of Education has 400 academic **staffs** and the other three institutions have a total of around 160 academic **staffs**." ★★★★★

# Stonecutter's Island

*n.*

**Definition:** a former island in Victoria Harbour, now part of the western Kowloon peninsula due to reclamation work. ★★★★★

# Suzie Wong

*idiomatic expression.*

**Definition:** a literary allusion to a character in the novel and movie, *The World of Suzie Wong*, by Richard Mason.

**Text example:**

> "Drive through Causeway Bay, the **Suzie Wong** district of Wanchai, and Happy Valley where the horse-racing tracks are located."

See: **yellow fever**.

**Note:** This term can be derogatory, since the fictional character was a prostitute who serviced foreigners. However, more recently, as marriage between Caucasians and Chinese has become more common and socially acceptable, the meaning may have become more lighthearted. ★★★☆☆

# swallow nest

*n.*

**Definition:** See: bird's nest.

**Text example:**

> "The first course at the dinner was Chinese **swallow-nest** soup." ★★★☆☆

# sycee

/saɪsiː/ *n.*

**Source language:** Cantonese (細絲).

**Definition:** ingots of high-quality silver bullion (archaic).

**Text example:**

"The importation of opium and exportation of **sycee** silver, both prohibited by imperial decree, were to become a major area of controversy in time." ⭐⭐⭐⭐

# T

tael
taikonaut
taipan
Tai Po
tai-tai
tai-tai lunch
tam
Tam Kung Festival
tang yuan
tea money
ten thousand steps
thousand-year egg
three-legged stool
tiffin
tin fong wife
Tin Hau
Tin Hau Festival
tin kau
tofu
Tolo Harbour
tong
tong fai
tong gau
tong lau
tong sui
tong yuen
triad
Tsim Sha Tsui
tsin
Tsing Yi (Island)
tso
Tsuen Wan
Tuen Mun
Tuen Ng
turnip
turnip cake

turtle's egg
typhoon signal number

# tael

/teɪl/ *n.*

**Source language:** Malay.

**Definition:** 1/16 of a catty.

**Text example:**

"As many of these dried food delicacies are very expensive, they are customarily priced in unit of **tael**. But the shops would display or show the prices in such a way that creates the impression the prices are for a catty."

See: **catty**.

★★★★☆

# taikonaut

/taɪkəʊnɔ:t/ *n.*

**Source languages:** Mandarin (太空人), Greek.

**Definition:** a Chinese astronaut/cosmonaut.

**Text example:**

"The Chief Executive, Mr Tung Chee Hwa, and China's first **taikonaut**, Mr Yang Liwei, officiated at the opening ceremony of the 'Exhibition on China's First Manned Space Mission' at the Hong Kong Science Museum."

★★★☆☆

# taipan

/taɪpan/ *n.*

**Source language:** Cantonese (大班).

**Definition:** the head of a large powerful business (largely archaic).

**Text example:**

"It had been used as the Russian Consul's office and subsequently the residence of Augustine Herd & Co.'s **taipans**."

**Note:** Currently mostly used for heads of long-established companies.

★★★★★

# Tai Po

/taɪ pəʊ/ *n.*

**Source language:** Cantonese (大埔).

**Definition:** a town and district in the eastern New Territories adjacent to Tolo Harbour; originally a market town. ★★★★★

# tai-tai

/taɪ taɪ/ *n.*

**Source language:** Cantonese (太太).

**Definition:** the idle wife of a rich man.

**Text example:**

"Did you hear that **tai-tai** Blimpy Li went to the beach in Florida and almost died of heat stroke? Fortunately the doctor got to her in time and opened her mink coat." ★★★★☆

# tai-tai lunch

*fixed expression.*

**Definition:** a social gathering (for lunch) of tai-tais.

**Text example:**

"Her description in November 1831 of a 'lady party,' which aptly equates with a '**tai-tai lunch**' in Hong Kong today, is one of the most appealing." ★☆☆☆☆

# tam

/dam/ *n.*

**Source language:** Cantonese (擔).

**Definition:** 100 catties or 1 picul (uncommon).

**Text example:**

1 picul (tam) = 100 catties. (largely archaic)

See: **catty.** ★★★★★

# Tam Kung Festival

/tam kuŋ festivəl/ *n.*

**Source languages:** Cantonese (譚公誕), English.

**Definition:** a non-statutory holiday to honor the birthday of a god of the sea, on the eighth day of the fourth month of the lunar calendar.

**Text example:**

"In 1984 more than forty flags bearing the distinctive Wo Shing Wo triad society logo were erected along Nathan Road—the main thoroughfare on the Kowloon peninsula—to draw attention to a dinner in a nearby restaurant, purportedly being held in celebration of the **Tam Kung festival**."

★★★☆☆

# tang yuan (also tong yuen)

/tɔŋ juːn/ *n.*

**Source language:** Cantonese (湯圓).

**Definition:** a sweet glutinous rice flour ball, often stuffed with peanut, sugar, red bean or sesame. It is traditionally eaten during the Lantern Festival.

**Text example:**

❶ "People eat Yuan Xiao or **Tang Yuan** which are balls of glutinous rice, sometimes rolled around a filling of sesame, peanuts, vegetables or meat. **Tang Yuan** are often cooked in red bean or other kinds of sweet soup. The round shape symbolizes wholeness and unity."

❷ "'**Tong yuens**' (*glutinous rice dumplings*) bring together the union of a happy and healthy family."

★★★★★

# tea money

*idiomatic expression.*

**Definition:** a euphemism for a corrupt payment.

**Text example:**

"He had to pay a man $30 as **tea money** (swindled) to get the license for him."

**Underlying conceptualization:** A BRIBE IS (MONEY FOR) A DRINK [TARGET DOMAIN ➡ CORRUPTION] [SOURCE DOMAIN ➡ FOOD].

# ten thousand steps

*fixed expression.*

**Definition:** physical exercise for health, a training program.

**Text example:**

"Walk Ten Thousand Steps for Health programme."

# thousand-year egg

*n.*

See: **century egg**.

# three-legged stool

*idiomatic expression.*

**Definition:** a political or economic situation dependent on three main aspects.

**Text example:**

"The most common diagnosis is that China's economy is 'unbalanced.' The **three-legged stool** of its GDP leans too much on exports and investment, and too little on consumption. All those exports and investments may be helping fast growth today, the argument goes, but they can't be relied on for tomorrow."

# tiffin

/tifin/ *n.*

**Source language:** Indian English.

**Definition:** lunch.

**Text example:**

"In some instances petty quarrels were the excuse ... for a strike, while in three cases the cause was a demand for hours of labour, i.e. from 7 to 5, with an hour for **tiffin**, as opposed to the native hours of 6 to 6, with no stated intervals for refreshment."

**Note:** The term *tiffin* is becoming less common in HKE, except for usage in some restaurants.

# tin fong wife

/tin fɔŋ waɪf/ *n.*
**Source language:** Cantonese (填房).
**Definition:** a new wife to fill the role of kit fat, after the first wife has died (archaic).
**Text example:**

"His story was that the girl had been properly married to him as his '**tin fong**' **wife**."

# Tin Hau

/tin haʊ/ *n.*
**Source language:** Cantonese (天后).
**Definition:** a local goddess.
**Text example:**

"**Tin Hau** is the goddess of the sea and is therefore considered an important deity in the fishing community."

# Tin Hau Festival

*n.*
**Source languages:** Cantonese (天后誕), English.
**Definition:** a non-statutory holiday to honor the birthday of the goddess of the sea, on the 23rd day of the third month in the lunar calendar.
**Text example:**

"The main feature of the **Tin Hau festival**, besides the usual obligatory opera performances, was a competition for the best floral shrine."

# tin kau

/tin gaʊ/ *n.*

**Source language:** Cantonese (天九).

**Definition:** a gambling game based on tiles.

**Text example:**

"I knew of young constables in the 80s who couldn't tell the difference between the sound of mahjong and **tin kau** tiles!"

# tofu

*idiomatic expression.*

**Source language:** Mandarin (豆腐).

**Definition:** construction of poor quality.

**Text example:**

"'**Tofu** buildings.' That's what rural Chinese have long called structures thrown up with remarkable speed. They look fine on the outside, but aren't much sturdier than the bean curd on last night's dinner table."

**Underlying conceptualization:** THE STRUCTURE OF BUILDINGS IS THE STRUCTURE OF FOOD (generic) [TARGET DOMAIN ➡ BUILDINGS] [SOURCE DOMAIN ➡ FOOD].

# Tolo Harbour

/təʊləʊ ˈhaːbə/ *n.*

**Source language:** Cantonese (吐露港).

**Definition:** a sheltered harbour adjacent to Tai Po in northeastern New Territories.

# tong (1)

/tɔŋ/ *n.*

**Source language:** Cantonese (黨).

**Definition:** a Chinese secret society (mostly archaic).

**Text example:**

"The outcome was the first purely Hong Kong secret

society, the Chung Wo **Tong**, or 'the Lodge of Loyalty and Righteousness,' which aspired to unite all local Triad members in support of Dr Sun's republican party."

See: **triad**.

# tong (2)

/tɔŋ/ *n.*

**Source language:** Cantonese (黨).

**Definition:** ❶ a meeting place for villagers in the New Territories (archaic); ❷ an arrangement of landownership in Chinese customary law for male heirs.

**Text example:**

❶ "They are the tso (literally means ancestors), the **tong** (hall of shrine), the yuen (encircled garden), and the wuei (the association)."

❷ "Its operation is limited only to non-exempted land in the New Territories which is registered in the name of or held for the benefit of a Chinese clan, family, **tong** or tso."

See: **tso**.

# tong fai

/tɔŋ faɪ/ *n.*

**Source language:** Cantonese (堂費).

**Definition:** a hall fee payable by pupils of subsidized school.

**Text example:**

"**Tong Fai** will be collected to support educational expenses at the same rate of $290 per year from the senior secondary students as in the previous year."

# tong gau

/tɔŋ gaʊ/ *n.*

**Source language:** (唐狗).

**Definition:** a local breed of dog.

**T**

**Text example:**

"Hong Kong currently kills 2,000 unwanted dogs and cats every month. These aren't just strays, your **tong gau**'s or ill animals. These are also pedigrees, puppies and healthy animals."

# tong lau

/tɔŋ laʊ/ *n.*

**Source language:** Cantonese (唐樓).

**Definition:** an old-style walk-up residential building.

**Text example:**

"How long a life a **tong lau** has depends on the quality of construction in the first place."

# tong sui

/tɔŋ sɔɪ/ *n.*

**Source language:** Cantonese (糖水).

**Definition:** a sweet dessert soup.

**Text example:**

"Hong Kongers like to finish a meal with a sweet, and that sweet is often chilled **tong sui** (sweet soup). It's the standard dessert fare in a Hakka restaurant. It's also popular as a snack."

# tong yuen

*n.*

See: **tang yuen**.

# triad

*n.*

**Definition:** ❶ a criminal gang; ❷ an anti-dynastic Chinese patriotic society often with a Buddhist religious mandate (archaic).

**Text example:**

❶ "Matthew was brought up in a poor single-parent family his father being a drug addict—and joined a **triad** society at the age of 13."

❷ "In its earlier phases the **Triad** Society was a Chinese secret society whose members, bound by oaths of blood brotherhood, were pledged to overthrow the foreign conquerors of their country and restore the ancient ruling house of China to the throne."

**Note:** The first meaning predominates in HKE today and describes organizations that are degenerations of societies as defined in ❷.

# Tsim Sha Tsui

/tsɪm ʃa tsɔɪ/ *n.*
**Source language:** Cantonese (尖沙咀).
**Definition:** a neighborhood in southern Yau Tsim Mong District, mostly reclaimed land, originally the site of Heung Po Tau Port.

# tsin

/tʃin/ *n.*
**Source language:** Chinese, dialect uncertain (錢).
**Definition:** 1/160 catty or 1 mace.
**Text example:**

"1 tsin or mace = 10 fan"

See: **catty**.

# Tsing Yi (Island)

/tsɪŋ ji:/ *n.*
**Source language:** Cantonese (青衣).
**Definition:** an island to the northwest of Hong Kong Island and south of Tsuen Wan; part of Kwai Tsing District. Reclamation work has enlarged the island's size.

# tso

*n.*

**Source language:** Cantonese.

**Definition:** ❶ ancestral estates under trust in old villages in the New Territories; ❷ ancestor.

**Text example:**

❶ "P is the registered manager of a Sham Kiu Ming **Tso** (the 'Tso') which is a Chinese ancestral worship trust. The premises known as the Remaining Portion … is held from the Government under lease in the name of the **Tso**."

❷ "They are the **tso** (literally means ancestors), the tong (hall of shrine), the yuen (encircled garden), and the wuei (the association)."

# Tsuen Wan

/tsuːn wɔːn/ *n.*

**Source language:** Cantonese (荃灣).

**Definition:** an industrial town and district in the southwestern New Territories, originally the site of the Sam Tung Uk Hakka village.

# Tuen Mun

/tuːn muːn/ *n.*

**Source language:** Cantonese (屯門).

**Definition:** a town and district in the southwestern New Territories, originally the site of Tsing Shan village.

# Tuen Ng

/duːn ŋ/ *n.*

**Source language:** Cantonese (端午).

**Definition:** a statutory holiday on the fifth day of the fifth month in the lunar calendar.

**Text example:**

"Dragon Boat Festival or **Tuen Ng**, which takes place in

early June (the fifth day of the fifth moon in the Chinese calendar), is a good time to be in Aberdeen." ★★★★☆

# turnip

*n.*

**Definition:** a large white (*daikon*) radish of the species, *Raphanus sativus* subsp. *Longipinnatus* and not a conventional turnip, which would be of the species *Brassica rapa* var. *rapa*.

**Text example:**

"Ingredients: Soba [buckwheat noodles] 200 g [7 oz], Diced green onion 1 tbsp, Daikon puree [**turnip** puree] 1 tbsp, Shredded toasted laver 1 tbsp, Wasabi 1/8 tsp."

★★★★☆

# turnip cake

*n.*

**Definition:** a food product that is made of radish and rice flour.

**Text example:**

"Before the Chinese New Year, my cousin, Jim and I help my mother prepare rice cakes and **turnip cakes**."

See: **turnip**. ★★★☆☆

# turtle's egg (also **turtle egg**)

*idiomatic expression.*

**Definition:** an insult, similar to "son-of-a-bitch."

**Text example:**

❶ "'Ma ti, that bastard son of a dog is certainly getting off light!' 'Drag the **turtle's egg** out of there and do him in right now!'"

❷ "Your Nicole **turtle egg** friend is coward and scared to come to help you." ★☆☆☆☆

# typhoon signal number

*fixed expression*.

**Definition:** a system of rating the strength of storms.

**Text example:**

> "**Typhoon Signal No.** 8 was hoisted on a Thursday and Sam was not required to return to work."

**Note:** The scale does not move consecutively from 1–10, but includes 1, 3, 8, 9, +10. ⭐⭐⭐⭐⭐

# U

uncle
unlucky draw

# uncle

*n.*

**Definition:** ❶ a friendly form of address for male persons above one's own age; ❷ any male parental friend or person of similar social status.

**Text example:**

> "To illustrate, let's assume there are two employees, **Uncle** Wah and Auntie Jane."

**Underlying conceptualizations:** A MEMBER OF SOCIETY IS A MEMBER OF THE FAMILY, A FRIEND OF THE PARENTS IS A MEMBER OF THE FAMILY [TARGET DOMAINS ➡ MEMBER OF SOCIETY, PARENTAL FRIEND] [SOURCE DOMAIN ➡ FAMILY].

See: **auntie**.

# unlucky draw

*fixed expression.*

**Definition:** a lottery for an unwanted result.

**Text example:**

> "A nurse at Queen Elizabeth Hospital has accused her department of being unfair by excluding senior nursing staff from the **unlucky draw** which determines who is put on standby for Sars patients."

# V

## Victoria Harbour vocabularies

# Victoria Harbour

*n.*

**Definition:** a deepwater harbor, sheltered from extreme storms by being located between Hong Kong Island and the Kowloon Peninsula. It was the focal point for the creation of the British colony.

# vocabularies

*n.*

**Definition:** words.

**Text example:**

"g-Smart i is also built-in with Office applications and a dictionary of 100,000 **vocabularies** with audio, new words expansion and book marking, offering greater flexibility on business."

# W

waah
wai
wallah wallah
Walled City
wan
Wan Chai
wan yee
wet market
white elephant
white gold
white tiger
winter congos
Wishing Tree
wok
Wong Tai Sin District
wonton
wuei
wushu

# waah (also wah)

/waː/ *interjection*.
**Source language:** Cantonese (嘩).
**Definition:** an exclamation, indicating surprise or amazement (usually verbal).
**Text example:**

❶ "**Waah** i just had my genetics midterm on Monday, and today the prof already told us that the results will be online tonite."

❷ "**Wah**! Here's the job for me."

# wai

/waɪ/ *fixed expression*.
**Source language:** Cantonese (喂).
**Definition:** a greeting (usually in spoken language, mostly used to answer a phone).
**Text example:**

"As he was almost ouside the door he hailed the shape—'**Wai**'—but got no response. By this time he was almost in the door and hailed again '**Wai**', walking toward the shape all the while."

# wallah wallah (also walla-walla)

/wɔlə wɔlə/ /wɔla wɔla/ *n*.
**Source language:** uncertain, possibly from Indian English or onomatopoeic for the engine sound.
**Definition:** a small boat used as a ferry for casual traffic (archaic).
**Text example:**

❶ "The key elements of the project are described as follows: reclamation and seawalls, roads and associated services, North Island Line Protection Works and Advance Trunk Road Tunnel (ATRT) for the CWB; reprovisioning of

Star Ferry Pier, public landing steps, **wallah wallah** moorings, and motor boat/launch operators' kiosks."

❷ "During the summer months, you can hire a small motorized **walla-walla** from Wong Shek Pier to take you to this dive location."

**walla walla** (drawing by Adrian Cennydd Petyt)

# Walled City

*n.*

See: **Kowloon Walled City**.

# wan (1)

/wɔn/ *n.*

**Source language:** Cantonese (灣).

**Definition:** an area.

**Text example:**

"'Sai wan,' 'Sheung **wan**.'"

**Note:** Usually used only in place names.

# wan (2)

/wɔn/ *n.*

**Source language:** Cantonese (灣).

**Definition:** a body of water partly enclosed by the shore, but with a wide opening to the sea; a bay.

**Text example:**

"Tai Long **Wan**, Hau Hoi **Wan**."

**Note:** Usually used only in place names.

# Wan Chai

/wan tʃaɪ/ *n.*

**Source language:** Cantonese (灣仔).

**Definition:** a district in the middle northern part of Hong Kong Island, location of the Handover ceremony and a red-light area.

## wan yee

/wən jiː/ *n.*

**Source language:** Cantonese (雲耳).

See: **black fungus**.

# wet market

*fixed expression.*

**Definition:** a market for selling fresh meat and fish, fruits and vegetables, sometimes locally produced.

**Text example:**

"Therefore, the challenge for Hong Kong is to give careful consideration of the function of **wet markets** against supermarkets, while providing training and education about safe food handling."

# white elephant

*fixed expression.*

**Definition:** an Asian symbol, denoting all kinds of powers and virtues.

**Text example:**

"A genuine **white elephant** is one of the most ancient signs of divine power and longevity in Chinese tradition—and Vietnamese and Indian and Thai and so on."

# white gold

*fixed expression.*

**Definition:** platinum and not a blend of silver and gold.

**Text example:**

"Misrepresentation Regarding Platinum. To rectify the ambiguities of the Chinese translation of 'platinum' and '**white gold**', we plan to amend paragraph 5(3) of the Trade Descriptions (Marking) (Gold and Gold Alloy) Order (Cap. 362A) to change the Chinese translation of **white gold**."

# white tiger

*idiomatic expression.*

**Definition:** a woman with a shaved pubic area.

**Text example:**

"Saw that she is really bare (**WHITE TIGER**) below not even stubble in sight."

# winter congos

*fixed expression.*

**Source languages:** Cantonese or Amoy dialect, English.

**Definition:** a variety of winter tea (archaic).

**Text example:**

"The Teas shipped by the vessels already alluded to, are of the latter description and would, had the monopoly continued, have been sent away in October and November next under the name Winter Teas' or 'Company **Winter Congos**.'"

# Wishing Tree

*n.*

**Definition:** a tree near Tai Po supposedly with magical qualities.

**Text example:**

"The **Wishing Tree** at Lam Tsuen ... is an attraction for locals for one major reason; the tree is reputed to make wishes come true."

**Note:** Because of damage caused to the tree, by the weight of too many wishes, wooden racks are now provided for the joss paper wishes to be hung.

**Wishing Tree** (drawing by Adrian Cennydd Petyt)

# wok

/wɔk/ *n.*

**Source language:** Cantonese (鑊).

**Definition:** ❶ trouble, problem (usually spoken language); ❷ a slang term for a satellite dish (usually spoken language).

**Text example:**

❶ "The dilemma was now on my table: the first **wok** to need attention. It was more than patching the **wok**; it was the preparation of the sort of stock exchange whose utility would become a crucial factor in maintaining Hong Kong as an international financial centre after 1997."

❷ "Thus a large trading company with a television 'dish' (**wok**) on the roof is known in Guangzhou as the 'trouble Company.'"

**Note:** This expression goes back to the Cantonese expression "to carry a black *wok*," meaning "trouble."

# Wong Tai Sin District

/wɔŋ taɪ sin 'distrikt/ *n.*

**Source language:** Cantonese (黃大仙).

**Definition:** a landlocked district in northeastern Kowloon peninsula, containing Wong Tai Sin Temple.

# wonton

/wɔntɔn/ *n.*

**Source language:** Cantonese (雲吞).

**Definition:** slang for "a used tissue typically with mucus from nose or throat" (usually spoken language).

**Text example:**

"GM asked me to look for that piece of paper in the bag. The bag had leftover lunch boxes, ice tea, afternoon tea, **wonton** (used tissue)."

# wuei

/wɔɪj/ *n.*

**Source language:** Cantonese (會).

**Definition:** a fraternal association.

See: **tso**.

# wushu

/wuːʃuː/ *n.*

**Source language:** Mandarin (武術).

**Definition:** a martial art similar to Kung fu.

**Text example:**

"If his **wu shu** medals at one level authenticate him, there are purists who question whether **wu shu** (designed for performance, not combat) is a 'proper' martial art."

★★★★★

# X

xiao long bao
XO sauce

# xiao long bao

/siːu luŋ baʊ/ *n.*

**Source language:** Mandarin (小籠包).

**Definition:** a type of dim sum made by wrapping a savory stuffing with a sheet of dough.

**Text example:**

"'If we need to find out how many **xiao long bao** we've sold, it would take weeks or even months to find out,' said Chow."

**Note:** Originated in Shanghai.

# XO sauce

/iks əʊ sɔːs/ *n.*

**Definition:** a prestigious seafood-based sauce often made with dried seafood cooked with chilli, onion, garlic and oil.

**Text example:**

"**XO Sauce** is a delicious snack on its own or it can be used to add a bit of flair to noodles, congee or dim sum."

# Y

Yau Ma Tei
Yau Tsim Mong District
ya-ya
yellow fever
yeuk
ye ye
yin-yang
yuan
Yue Lan
yuen
Yuen Long
yum cha
yum cha house
yum sing
yum-yum girl

# Yau Ma Tei

/jaʊ ma teɪ/ *n.*

**Source language:** Cantonese (油麻地).

**Definition:** a neighborhood in central Yau Tsim Mong District, originally a village.

⭐⭐⭐⭐⭐

# Yau Tsim Mong District

/jaʊtsimmɔŋ ˈdistrikt/ *n.*

**Source language:** Cantonese (油尖旺), English.

**Definition:** a district in the southwestern Kowloon peninsula, comprising the component parts Yau Ma Tei, Tsim Sha Tsui, and Mong Kok.

⭐⭐⭐⭐⭐

# ya-ya

/jæ jæ/ *n.*

**Source language:** Philippine English.

**Definition:** a female domestic servant.

**Text example:**

"Amah, Helper, **Ya-ya**, Auntie, Maid—they go by different labels but they're the glue that keeps Hong Kong together."

⭐☆☆☆☆

# yellow fever

*idiomatic expression.*

**Definition:** a sexual desire by Western men for Asian/Chinese women.

**Text example:**

"I watched the never-ending stream of hookers flowing into the bars. From a purely aesthetic point of view, very few of them are really pretty—most are relying on a combination of beer goggles and **yellow fever**."

See: **Suzie Wong**.

⭐⭐⭐☆☆

# yeuk

*n.*

**Source language:** Cantonese (archaic).

**Definition:** a part of a city, similar to ward or district (archaic).

**Text example:**

"The third **yeuk**: Sai Ying Pun."

# ye ye

/jiː jiː/ *n.*

**Source language:** Cantonese (爺爺).

**Definition:** paternal grandfather.

**Text example:**

"After their departure, Father would talk to **Ye Ye** alone for hours and hours in their office."

# yin-yang (also yuen yen, yuan yang)

/jin jæŋ/ *idiomatic expression.*

**Source language:** Mandarin (鴛鴦).

**Definition:** a blend of tea and coffee.

**Text example:**

❶ "A creamy coffee-tea combo, called '**yin-yang**,' is a popular refreshment."

❷ "These are all over the place, especially in Kowloon serving all kinds of frothy and sweet tea beverages, including **yuen yen** (a blend of coffee and tea)."

❸ "**Yuan yang** (coffee : tea)."

# yuan

/juːan/ *n.*

**Source language:** Mandarin (圓).

**Definition:** Chinese currency, equivalent to the Renminbi.

**Text example:**

"The standard unit of currency in China is the renminbi (RMB), also known as the **yuan**."

See: **Renminbi** and **jiao**.

# Yue Lan

/juː lan/ *n.*

**Source language:** Cantonese (盂蘭).

**Definition:** a non-statutory holiday to honor the dead on the seventh month in the Chinese lunar calendar, on the fifteenth day.

**Text example:**

"The main festivities in the Buddhist calendar are the birthdays of Kwan-yin, goddess of fecundity and mercy, and **Yue Lan**, the Festival of Hungry Souls. The ... Hungry Ghost Festival is ... observed on the fifteenth day of the seventh lunar month ... Believers conceive of souls as hungry and thirsty, restless and plagued with desire, who can bring misery to earthly beings if not placated."

**Underlying conceptualizations:** A SUPERNATURAL BEING IS A HUMAN BEING, A DECEASED MEMBER OF THE COMMUNITY IS A SUPERNATURAL BEING [TARGET DOMAIN ➡ SUPERNATURAL BEING] [SOURCE DOMAIN ➡ HUMAN BEING].

See: **tso**.

# yuen

/juːn/ *n.*

**Source language:** Cantonese (園).

**Definition:** a garden in a traditional Chinese style.

**Text example:**

"Lung Tsai Ng **Yuen** is surely one of the most surprising places in Hong Kong's countryside—a Chinese landscaped garden set in the hills of southwest Lantau Island, accessible only by hiking."

# Yuen Long

/juːn lɔŋ/ *n.*

**Source language:** Cantonese (元朗).

**Definition:** a town and district in the northwestern New Territories adjacent to the Mainland border, originally a market town. ⭐⭐⭐⭐⭐

# yum cha

/jʌm tʃaː/ *v.*

**Source language:** Cantonese (飲茶).

**Definition:** ❶ to have teatime in a Chinese style; ❷ to drink tea.

**Text example:**

❶ "Although **yum cha** and dim sum are used synonymously in Hong Kong. There is, properly, a distinction—when you go to a restaurant to **yum cha**, you eat dim sum or, when you **yum cha** you drink tea and eat dim sum."

❷ "**Yum cha**, a term in Cantonese, literally meaning 'drinking tea,' refers to the custom of eating small servings of different foods while sipping Chinese tea ..." ⭐⭐⭐⭐☆

**yum cha** (drawing by Adrian Cennydd Petyt)

# yum cha house

*fixed expression.*

**Definition:** a restaurant that specializes in yum cha.

**Text example:**

"The closest thing you'll find is a **yum cha house**, or a dai pai dong."

See: **dai pai dong**.

# yum sing (also yum seng)

/jʌm səŋ/ *fixed expression.*

**Source language:** Cantonese (飲勝).

**Definition:** a cheer made before drinking an alcoholic beverage, popular at weddings.

**Text example:**

❶ "Between the many courses of the wedding banquet, a guest would leap up from his chair, shout '**Yum-Sing**! Good health!' to the bride and groom, and down his generous measure of French brandy in a gulp."

❷ "**Yum seng**. Cheers."

# yum-yum girl

/jʌm jʌm gɜːl/ *idiomatic expression.*

**Definition:** bar girl, prostitute.

**Text example:**

"The pick-up bars still line the road, **yum-yum girls** luring passers-by into their neon-lit dens, but these are the illegitimate daughters of Suzie Wong, not of Chinese but Thai descent, wearing not elegant silk cheongsams but cheap miniskirts raised to immodest heights."

See: **Suzie Wong**.

# Appendices

# Cultural Conceptualizations

## *Target domains*

### BUILDINGS

| | |
|---|---|
| THE STRUCTURE OF BUILDINGS IS THE STRUCTURE OF FOOD | ➡ **tofu buildings** |

### CORRUPTION

| | |
|---|---|
| A BRIBE IS (MONEY FOR) A DRINK | ➡ **tea money** |
| A BRIBE IS A GIFT | ➡ **lai see, lucky money** |

### DECEASED MEMBER OF THE COMMUNITY

| | |
|---|---|
| A DECEASED MEMBER OF THE COMMUNITY IS A SUPERNATURAL BEING | ➡ **ghost** |

### FELLOW MEMBER OF A SOCIAL GROUP

| | |
|---|---|
| A FELLOW MEMBER OF A SOCIAL GROUP ONE BELONGS TO IS A SIBLING | ➡ **big brother, big sister, school brother/sister** |

### MEMBER OF SOCIETY

| | |
|---|---|
| A MEMBER OF SOCIETY IS A MEMBER OF THE FAMILY | ➡ **auntie, uncle** |

### OCCUPATION

| | |
|---|---|
| A JOB IS A FOOD CONTAINER | ➡ **golden rice bowl, iron rice bowl** |

---

PAPER MODEL

---

A PAPER MODEL IS A REAL OBJECT
IN THE SUPERNATURAL WORLD ➡ **hell bank notes,
paper money,
spirit money, joss paper**

---

PARENTAL FRIEND

---

A FRIEND OF THE PARENTS IS
A MEMBER OF THE FAMILY ➡ **auntie, uncle**

---

SALARY

---

SALARY IS FOOD

EQUAL PAY IS EATING FROM THE
SAME FOOD CONTAINER ➡ **one big pot wages**

---

SEX

---

SEX IS RIDING

THE PERSON WHO ARRANGES SEX
IS A STABLE BOY ➡ **mafoo (mafu)**

---

SWEET SMELL

---

A SMELL IS A VALUABLE OBJECT IN THE
SUPERNATURAL WORLD ➡ **joss stick**

---

SUPERNATURAL BEING

---

A SUPERNATURAL BEING IS
A HUMAN BEING ➡ **"ghosts" like watching
this type of performance,
Hungry Ghost Festival**

## *Source domains*

---

FAMILY

---

➡ PARENTAL FRIEND
➡ FELLOW MEMBER OF A SOCIAL GROUP
➡ MEMBER OF SOCIETY

---

FOOD

---

➡ CORRUPTION
➡ OCCUPATION
➡ BUILDINGS

---

FOOD CONTAINER

---

➡ OCCUPATION
➡ SALARY

---

GIFT

---

➡ CORRUPTION

---

HUMAN BEING

---

➡ SUPERNATURAL BEING

---

OBJECT IN THE SUPERNATURAL WORLD

---

➡ PAPER MODEL
➡ A SWEET SMELL

---

RIDING

---

➡ SEX

# Name Changes in Hong Kong and Neighboring Asia

No claim is made that the list below is exhaustive, or that any term is more authentic than the other. The more commonly used term in Hong Kong English is listed first and other terms are listed after it.

The following changes or variations are not included. (1) There was a massive mandated Hong Kong name change regime under Japanese rule. However, the names have not been used after the Second World War, so these names are not recorded here. (2) A number of organizations dropped the prefix "Royal" from their names at the time of the handover. These changes are also not being noted, since that is an accurate change of description, rather than a real name change. (3) Likewise, description changes are not included, for example: Hung Hom Bay to Hung Hom (the area). (4) Different romanization systems have created different spellings for Chinese words and place names. These orthographic differences cannot be considered changes and are also not included.

Not in all cases do the changed names refer to exactly the same area as before. Some place names cover related, but larger or smaller areas. For example, Vietnam, Laos, and Cambodia used to be part of French Indochina, which in turn used to be a Chinese vassal state. For Hong Kong, Apliu Street and Apliu Village can serve as an example.

Obvious nicknames are put in quotation marks. Sometimes the difference between names and nicknames is not clear.

Where a name is used with or without a part, such as Stanley (Bay)/Chek Chue (Wan), the variable part is put in brackets. Some information is added in triangular brackets, for example: Quarry Bay <western side>/Lai Chi.

Hong Kong has been spared some stress and confusion because Beijing took the mature decision not to go around changing colonial names, like Aberdeen, King's Road, or Queen Elizabeth Hospital. The Chinese government recognized that there is a colonial past and did not try to rewrite history in the form of place names, as happened in other cases.

### *Name, alternative name(s)*

**General**

Big Wave Bay/Tai Long Wan <multiple sites>
Hong Kong/Fragrant Harbour/Xianggang/San-on district
Hong Kong International Airport/Chek Lap Kok Airport/
Hong Kong International Airport/ Kai Tak Airport <the old HK airport in Kowloon City before Chek Lap Kok began operation in 1997>
Kowloon City/Kwun Fu Cheng

**Hong Kong Island**

Aberdeen/Heung Gong Tsai/Little Fragrant Harbour

Bank Street/Wardley Street

Brick Hill/Nam Long Shan

"Cat Street Market"/Upper Lascar Row in Sheung Wan

Catchick Street/Chater Street

Causeway Bay/Tung Lo Wan

Central/Victoria/Chung Wan

Chai Wan/Sai Wan

Chinese People's Liberation Army Forces Hong Kong Building/Prince of Wales Building

Collinson, Cape/Hak Kok Tau

Court of Final Appeal/Supreme Court

Court of Final Appeal Building/<former> French Mission Building

Des Voeux Road/Bowring Praya

Happy Valley/Wong Nai Chung Valley/Pau Ma Tei

Hollywood Road/Man Mao Temple Straight Road

Jardine House/Connaught Centre

Jervois Street/Su-hang Street

Johnston Road/Praya East

Kennedy Road/Albany Lane

Legislative Council Building/<former> Supreme Court Building

Magazine Island/Fo Yeuk Chau

Middle Island/Tong Po Chau

Mount Davis/Mo Sing Leng

Mount Parker/Pak Ka Shan/Lam San Ting

Po Yan Street/Cemetery Street/Fan Mo Street

Quarry Bay <western side>/Lai Chi

Queen's Road Central/"Concubine Lane"

Repulse Bay/Tsin Shui Wan

Sacred Heart Canossian College/Sacred Heart School/Italian Convent School
Shau Kei Wan/Starvation Bay/Basket Cleaning Bay
Shek O (Wan)/Rocky
Shek Tong Tsui/Western Quarry/West Point
Stanley (Bay)/Chek Chue (Wan)
Sulphur Channel/Lau Wong Hoi Hap
Tai Ping Shan area/Chinatown
Tai Wong Street East/Lyall's Lane
Telegraph Bay/Kong Sin Wan/Tai Hau Wan
Tsat Tsz Mui Road/"Seven Sisters"
The Twins/Ma Kong Shan
Victoria Road/Victoria Jubilee Road
Violet Hill/Tsz Lo Lan Shan
Wan Chai/Spring Garden/Ha Wan
Wing Lok Street Wharf/"The Triangular Wharf"

**New Kowloon**

Apliu Street/Apliu Village
Beacon Hill/Pat Ka Shan
Broadcast Drive/Lung Cheung Road
Diamond Hill/Tsuen Shek Shan
Kai Tak Nullah/Long Jin River
Kowloon Peak/Fei Ngo Shan
Kwai Fong/Lap Sap Wan/Refuse Bay/Gin Drinker's Bay
Lam Tin/Ham Tin Shan
Lion Rock/Sz Tsz Shan
Lok Fu/Lo Fu Ngam
Tai Wo Hau/Lo Uk Cheung
Temple Hill/Tsz Wan Shan
Ying Wa College/Anglo-Chinese College

## Kowloon

Austin Station/West Kowloon Station/Canton Road Station

Boundary Street/Chungking Street/New Chwang Street/Praya Street

Bowring Street/Eighth Street

Canton Road/MacDonnell Road

Changsha Street/Tientsin Street/Hill Street

Chatham Road/Des Voeux Road

Ching Yi To Barracks <a part of the Hong Kong Barracks>/Queen's Line

Fa Yuen Street/"Garden Street"/"Sport Shoe Street"/"Sneakers Street"

Fuk Tsun Street/Fuk Tsun Heung Main Street

Haiphong Road/Elgin Road

Hankow Road/Garden Road

Hanoi Road/East Road

Hart Avenue/Sainam Avenue

Hung Hom Station/Kowloon Station

Hok Yuen Street/Hok Yuen Road

Hong Lok Street/"Bird Street"

Jordan Road/Sixth Street

Junction Road Christian Cemetery/Pak Hok Shan

Kai Tak Tunnel/Airport Tunnel

Kansu Street/First Street

King George V Memorial Park <in Jordan>/Kwun Chung Hill

Kowloon Bay/Ngau Tau Kok Industrial Area

The Lantau Link/Lantau Fixed Crossing

Nanking Street/Fifth Street

Nanning Lane/Third Lane <since eliminated>

Nathan Road/Robinson Road

Nathan Road <in Tsim Sha Tsui>/"The Golden Mile"

Nelson Street/"Old Book Street"
Ning Po Street/Fourth Street
Observatory Hill/Mount Elgin
Pakhoi Street/Second Street
Peking Road/Chater Street
Saigon Street/Third Street
Shanghai Street/Police Station Street
Shantung Lane/Nullah Lane
Sheung On Lane/Sheung On Street
Signal Hill/Blackhead Hill
Stonecutter's "Island"/Ngong Shuen Chau
Suchow Lane/Fuk Shing Lane
Taku Street/Foochow Street/Station Street
Tai Yuen Street/"Toy Street"
Temple Street/"Men's Street"
Tientsin Street <eliminated>
Tung Choi Street/"Woman's Street"/"Ladies Street"
    /"Lady's Street"
Tung Chou Street/Foochow Street
Yunnan Lane/Seventh Lane/"Letter Writing Street"
Woosung Street/Kennedy Street
Wuchow Terrace/East Terrace <since eliminated>
Wuhu Street/Market Street/Main Street

**New Territories**

Amah Rock/Mong Fu Shek
Basalt Island/Fo Shek Chau
Black Hill/Ng Kwai Shan
Bluff Island/Sha Tong Hau Shan
Bolder Point/Pak Kok
Buffalo Hill/Shui Ngau Shan
Castle Peak/Tuen Mun Shan
Castle Peak Bay/Tuen Mun Bay

Castle Rock/Lo Chau Pak Pai

Cheung Chau/"Dumbbell Island"

Chung Ying Street/The Border Street

Clear Water Bay/Tsing Shui Wan

Coral Beach/Tung Wan Tsai/"Lap Sap Beach"

Crossroads International/Perowne Barracks

Deep Bay/Hau Hoi Wan

Discovery Bay/Disco Bay/D-Bay/DB/Tai Pak Wan/
    Yi Pak Wan

Disneyland/Penny's Bay/Chok Ko Wan

Double Haven/Yan Chau Tong

East Lamma Channel/Tung Pok Liu Hoi Hap

George Island/Luk Chau

Gold Coast/Gordon Hard

Gruff Head/Heung Lo Kok

Harbour Island/Pak Sha Tau Chau

Hebe Haven/Pak Sha Wan

High Island/Leung Shuen Wan Chau

High Junk Peak/Tiu Yue Yung

The Hunchbacks/Ngau Ngak Shan

Joss House Bay/Tai Miu Wan

Junk Bay/Tseung Kwan O

Junk Island/Fat Tong Chau

Kat O (Chau)/Crooked Island

Kat O Hoi/Crooked Harbour

Lamma Island/Pok Liu Chau

Lantau Island/Tai Yu Shan/Nam Tao Island

Lantau Peak/Fung Wong Shan

Long Harbour/Tai Tan Hoi

Middle Channel/Chek Chau Hau

Mirs Bay/Tai Pang Wan

Morning Beach/Nam Tam Wan

Mount Hallowes/Tam Chai Shan

Ninepin Group/Kwo Chau (Kwan To)

North Channel/Tai Chek Mun
Pak Chau/Tree Island
Pillar Point/Mong Hau Shek
Ping Chau/Peng Chau[1]
Plover Cove/Shuen Wan (Hoi)
Port Shelter/Ngau Mei Hoi
Razor Hill/Che Kwu Shan
Rocky Harbour/Leung Shuen Wan Hoi
Sai Kung Hoi/Inner Port Shelter
Sharp Island/Kiu Tsui Chau
Sharp Peak/Nam She Tsim
Shayuyong/Sha Yue Chung
Shelter Island/Ngau Mei Chau
Shenzhen River/Sham Chun River
Shing Mun Reservoir/Jubilee Reservoir
Sok Kwu Wan/Picnic Bay
Starling Inlet/Sha Tau Kok Hoi
Steep Island/Ching Chau
Sunshine Island/Chau Kung To
Table Island/Ping Min Chau
Tai Wo/Tai Po New Market
Tap Mun Chau/Grass Island
Tathong Channel/Lam Tong Hoi Hap
Tathong Point/Nam Tong Mei
Three Fathoms Cove/Kei Ling Ha Hoi
Tide Cove/Shatin Harbour/Shatin Hoi
Tiu King Leng/Tiu Keng Leng/Rennie's Mill/
    "Hanging (neck) Ridge"
Tolo Channel/Chek Mun Hoi Hap
Tolo Harbour/Tai Po Harbour/Tai Po Hoi
Tsing Yi North Bridge/Tsing-Tsuen Bridge
Trio Island/Tai Lak Lei
University KCR Station/Ma Liu Shui KCR Station
West Lamma Channel/Sai Pok Liu Hoi Hap

## *Other places in Eastern and Southern Asia*

Amoy/Xiamen

Andong/Dandong

Bangalore/Bengaluru

Bangladesh/East Pakistan

Baroda/Vadodra

Beijing/Peking

Borneo/Kalimantan

Burma/Myanmar

Calicut/Kozhikode

Cambodia <kingdom of>/Kampuchea <People's Republic of>

Chennai/Madras

Chungking/Chongqing

Cochin/Kochi

Crooked Harbour/Kat O Hoi

Crooked Island/Kat O Chau

Daliang/Kaifeng/Bianjing

Diaoyutai/Senkaku (Islands)

Dutch/Netherlands New Guinea/Papua/West New Guinea/West Papua/Irian Jaya/Irian Barat <not to be confused with Papua New Guinea, which is the eastern half of the same island>

East Timor/Timor-Leste/Portuguese Timor

Guangdong/Guangzhou[2]/Canton/Kwangtung

Hebei/Zhili

Indonesia/Dutch/Netherlands East Indies

Jakarta/Djakarta/Batavia/Jayakarta/Sunda Kelapa

Kannur/Cannanore

Kanpur/Cawnpore

Kirin province/Jilin province

Klang: See Port Klang

Kolkata/Calcutta/Fort William

Korea/Joseon/Goryeo
Kwantung Leased Territory/Guandongzhou
Liaoning/Fengtian
Macau/University of/University of East Asia
Mainland Southeast Asia <Vietnam-Laos-Cambodia>/
    Indochina/French Indochina
Malaysia/Federation of Malaya/Langkasuka
Manchuria/North East China <Heilongjiang and
    Jilin>/Manchukuo
Mongolia/Inner Mongolia/Nei Mongol
Mumbai/Bombay
Pathein/Bassein
Port Klang/Port Swettenham
Pu-er/Simao
Qinghai/Kokonor
Rangoon/Yangon/Dagon
Sabah/British North Borneo
Saigon/Ho Chi Minh City
Seoul/Hanyang/Hanseong
Shantou/Swatow
Singapore/Temasek
Songjin/Kimchaek
Southern Vietnam/Cochinchina
Taiwan/Republic of China/Formosa/province of
    Taiwan
Thailand/Siam
Tibet/Shangri-La[3]/Xizang Zizhiqu
Tokyo/Edo
Xi'an/Chang'an
Xinjiang Uygur/Sinkiang/East Turkestan/Chinese
    Turkestan/Uyghuristan
Yangtze River/Chang Jiang
Yellow River/Huang He River

Yinxu/Anyang

Zhongshan (Central Mountain)/Heungshan
   (Fragrant Mountain)

**Notes:**

[1] There are two different islands with the name Peng Chau. The smaller one is often written as Ping Chau in English to avoid confusion.

[2] The English term "Canton" has been used for both the province of Guangdong and the city of Guangzhou.

[3] Shangri-La is fictional and not unambiguously only associated with Tibet.

# Hong Kong English Words Now Used Internationally

The following English words are from Hong Kong and Chinese English, but are now commonly used in other varieties of English. Most of these words have not been included in the dictionary, since they are in such common use outside of Hong Kong. Those that do have an entry in the dictionary have a different pronunciation in HKE, as in the case of *chow mein*, or a different spelling, as in the case of *fung shui*. Some of these words or expressions have a secondary meaning in HKE, such as *wonton*. Others like *Cultural Revolution* are from Mainland China, but the word has been transmitted to the world through HKE.

**acupuncture**: a treatment for pain by inserting the tips of needles at specific nerve nodes

**barefoot doctor**: a lay health care worker, especially in revolutionary rural China, providing first aid, basic medical care, midwifery and preventive medicine

**beggar's chicken**: a chicken dish cooked wrapped in lotus leaves and clay

**bitter melon**: the bitter tasting gourd from a vine of the species *Momordica charantia*

**capitalist roader**: in Maoist political theory, a communist person or group who wishes to uses capitalist methods to achieve communist goals

**chase the dragon**: smoking opium

**chi**: psychic energy

**chop suey**: a meat and vegetable rice-based dish of Cantonese origin

**chopsticks**: tableware consisting of a pair of sticks used to eat food with

**Confucius**: a Chinese philosopher (circa 551–478 BC) (also **Confucian**; **Confucianism**)

**Cultural Revolution**: ❶ a radical social reform in China initiated by Mao Zedong in 1965 and carried out by the Red Guards resulting in violent purges of intellectuals and socio-economic chaos; ❷ a lighthearted description of a major change in fashion or society (a sense which is not socially acceptable in Hong Kong)

**dead cat bounce**: a small, brief recovery in the price of a declining stock.

**dragon dance**: a dance performed by many people with a very long dragon costume

**egg fu yung**: a Cantonese-style farmer's omelette

**face** (to save/lose): status held in the opinion of others

**feng shui**: a traditional system of esthetics by means of geographic features

**ginseng**: a herb believed by some to have medicinal powers

**gung-ho**: to be very enthusiastic and dedicated

**I Ching**: an ancient Chinese manual of divination

**ketchup**: a thick tomato sauce, originally an Amoy fish sauce

**kumquat**: a small oval citrus fruit with thin sweet rind and very acid pulp or a tree that produces such a fruit

**kung-fu**: a Chinese martial art, with associations in myth and legend

**la mein**: a variety of pulled noodles

**lemon**[1]: a yellow oval fruit with acidic flesh and the tree which produces it

**lion dance**: a traditional Chinese dance

**lo pan**, also **lou pan**, **luo pan**: a Feng Shui compass.
   **Note:** Not to be confused with *Lo-pan*, the patron God
   of Carpenters

**loquat**: a small yellow subtropical fruit with a large stone

**lychee**: a fruit with a thin rigid skin enclosing a sweet pulp
   and a single seed

**mandarin**, *fruit*: a loose-skinned variety of orange

**Mandarin**, *language*: the dialect spoken in Beijing and
   the origin of Putonghua

**mandarin**, *official*: a senior government official of
   imperial China

**Middle Kingdom**: the country of China

**money tree**: a tree which is reputed to offer good luck, or
   any tree sold as a money tree

**Monkey King**: Sun Wukong, a character in the classical
   novel *The Journey to the West*

**napa cabbage**: a vegetable of the species *Brassica rapa*
   subsp. *pekinensis*

**paper tiger**: in Maoist political theory, a person or
   organization that appears powerful but is really powerless

**Peking duck**: a type of roasted duck, the best of which
   are made in Hong Kong, not Beijing

**pidgin**: a form of language used for trade between
   people without a common language

**potsticker**: a steamed or fried dough wrapped food filled
   with meat or vegetables

**Red Guards**: in Maoist political thought, young extreme-
   communist political enforcers

**running dog**: in Maoist political thought, a submissive
   follower of a different political system

**Shanghai** (*v.*): illegal forced service on a ship, often by
   kidnapping a drugged victim

**sifu**: a teacher, often used in Daoism or martial arts

**Son of Heaven**: the emperor of China

**spring roll**: chopped vegetables wrapped in thin dough and fried

**squeeze**: a corrupt payment obtained by coercion or intimidation

**tai chi**: a martial art based on sequences of slow controlled actions, often used for relaxation and balance and health

**tea**: a beverage made by steeping the dried leaves of the tea plant in hot water (also a small afternoon meal which includes tea)

**tea eggs**: a type of boiled eggs produced by a Hong Kong method

**tofu**: a curd made from soybeans

**tycoon**: a wealthy and powerful businessman

**typhoon**: a cyclonic tropical storm occurring in the China sea

**warlord**: an unaccountable military leader exercising civil power

**winter melon**: a large white-fleshed melon that is the fruit of *Benincasa hispida*

**wok**: a traditional convex frying pan

**wonton**: a type of dim sum filled with spiced minced pork, served in soup

**ying yang**: a philosophical description of how balanced opposing concepts, such as light and dark, are interdependent in the natural world

**yu**: fish

**Zen**: A Buddhist school of enlightenment through meditation

**Note:**

[1] The origin of the word *lemon* is uncertain, but may possibly be from Cantonese.

# Sources for the Text Examples

Several examples were collected for each dictionary entry. Included in this list are the sources selected to be used for the text examples with each entry. Website URLs may change, but the listed source was active when the glossary was being prepared.

**ABC**: Anna Wu, Chairperson, Equal Opportunities Commission, "Management: Competencies and current perspectives, corporate responsibilities in the area of human rights," http://www.eoc.org.hk/eoc/GraphicsFolder/SpeechContent.aspx?itemid=5088.

**acting-up**: http://www.edb.org.hk/EDNEWHP/resource/edu_doc/coa/sec_coa/App03.htm.

**ah-ba**: www.theology.org.hk/shalom/2001jan_eng/0101_eng.htm.

**ah-cha**: Yau Ching, *Filming Margins: Tang Shu Shuen, a Forgotten Hong Kong Woman Director* (Hong Kong: Hong Kong University Press, 2004), p. 242.

**aided school**: Hugh Witt (ed.), *Hong Kong Yearbook 1993: A Review of 1992* (Hong Kong: Government Printer, 1993), p. 121.

**aiyeeah**, also **ayah**: ❶ Nury Vittachi, *Asian Values* (Hong Kong: Chameleon Press, 1996), p. 38. ❷ May Holdsworth (with additional text by Caroline Courtauld), *Foreign Devils:*

*Expatriates in Hong Kong* (Oxford: Oxford University Press, 2002), p. 51.

**alphabets**: LegCo Panel on Education, "Minutes of meeting, held on Monday, May 21, 2001 at 4:30 pm," LC Paper No. CB(2)2329/00-01.

**amah**: Betty Wei and Elizabeth Li, *Culture Shock! Hong Kong: A Survival Guide to Customs and Etiquette*, second edition (Singapore, Times Books International, 1998), p. 78.

**A quality**: The Independent Commission Against Corruption (ICAC), "Going Dutch or what about zero tolerance on corruption?" (2003), http://www.icac.org.hk/symposium/2003/Presentation/Day1/Ensuring%20Police%20Integrity%20 (Dick%20Pijl%20-%20Speech).pdf.

**A share**: Bruce Herschensohn (ed.), *Hong Kong at the Handover* (Lanham: Lexington Books, 2000), p. 126.

**astronaut**: May Holdsworth (with additional text by Caroline Courtauld), *Foreign Devils: Expatriates in Hong Kong* (Oxford: Oxford University Press, 2002), p. 210.

**auntie**, **aunty**: ❶ Cherrie Chan Shuk Mei, "Another World," http://www.cuhk.edu.hk/eng/publications/CUWritingIV.pdf. ❷ Dino Mahoney, "Songbirds: 'Brother-sister, sister-brother' Part 2. Radio Television Hong Kong, Radio 4 (2004), http://rthk.hk/classicschannel/download/brother02.pdf.

**auntie (visiting, coming)**: The Bachelor's Swan Song, http://www.brns.com/pages4/maggie3.html.

**ayah**: see **amah**.

**bai san**: ❶ Nury Vittachi, *Reliable Sauce: The Secret Diaries of Lai See* (Hong Kong: Pacific Century Books, 1991), p. 125. ❷ *OffBeat*, "Geomantic considerations" (August 13–26, 1997): http://www.police.gov.hk/offbeat/613/news2.html.

**bak choi**: see **bok choy**.

**bamboo snake**: Stephen J. Karsen, Michael Wai-neg Lau, and Anthony Bogadek, *Hong Kong Amphibians and Reptiles* (Hong Kong: Provisional Urban Council, 1998), p. 148.

**banana**: Solomon Leong, "Code-mixing, 'race' and 'whiteness': A triangulated analysis of the Neutrogena advertisement." *Perspectives: Working Papers in English and Communication*, 16(1) (2004): 118, http://www.cityu.edu.hk/en/research/sleong.pdf.

**ban mui**: Cecile Torda Lowe, "Migrant workers: The excluded 'others' in a globalising world: The case of the Filipino domestic workers in Hong Kong" (2007), http://inter-disciplinary.net/ati/diversity/pluralism/pl3/Lowe%20paper.pdf, p. 7.

**bashi hou**: The Dark Side, "The other side of Hong Kong: Our brave new generation of hooligans" (2010), http://thedarkside.hk/2010/01/07/our-brave-new-generation-of-hooligans/.

**BBC**: see **ABC**.

**Beida**: Che-po Chan, *Political Pragmatism on the Chinese Campus Since 1989* (Hong Kong: Faculty of Social Sciences, Lingnan College, 1996), p. 12.

**big brother**: ❶ Mathew Lui, "A bad student

turned out to be …," CCC Kung Lee College, (n.d.), http://www.hkbu.edu.hk/~ccd/Publications/P050946-ccd-news-a4%20(8-10).pdf. ❷ Education Bureau (formerly Education and Manpower Bureau), "Whole-school approach to integrated education" (n.d.), http://www.emb.gov.hk/index.aspx?nodeID=185&langno=1.

**big sister**: see **big brother**.

**bird's nest**: Shun Wan Chan, "Review of scientific research on edible bird's nest" (2006), http://www.hkfsta.com.hk/articles/special/article7.htm.

**black fungus**: Joyce Kam, "Hearty fare for holidays." *The Standard* (January 13, 2009), http://www.thestandard.com.hk/news_detail.asp?we_cat=16&art_id=76907&sid=22216022&con_type=3&d_str=20090113&fc=3.

**boat congee**: The Government of Hong Kong Special Administrative Region, Food and Environmental Hygiene Department, Risk Assessment Studies, Report No. 22, nutrient values of indigenous congee, rice and noodle dishes, Annex V (2006).

**BoHo**: Richard Sterling, Elizabeth Chong, and Lushan Charles Qin, *World Food Hong Kong (Lonely Planet World Food Guides)* (Footscray, Victoria: Lonely Planet Publications, 2001), p. 159.

**boiled egg**: Lawrence Gray, "Soft boiled egg." The Hong Kong Writers' Circle (n.d.), http://www.hkwriterscircle.com/members_more.php?id=498_0_8_0_M.

**bok choy**, also **bak choi**, **pak choi**, **pak choy**:
❶ The Government of the Hong Kong Special Administrative Region, Department of Health EatSmart website (n.d.), http://www.eatsmart.gov.hk/eng/template/indexe086.html?pid=231&id=227. ❷ Hong Kong Tourism Board, "Vegetarian cuisine in Hong Kong: Vegetarian restaurants, Chinese vegetarian food" (2008), http://www.beta.discoverhongkong.com/eng/dining/chinese-vegetarian-cuisine.html. ❸ Pang Wing Chi, Heep Woh College, The Hong Kong Tuberculosis Chest and Heart Diseases Association, "Heart healthy eating, winning recipes and comments: Student competition champion" (2002). ❹ Food and Nutritional Sciences Programme, The Chinese University of Hong Kong, "Fun-In-Seven" (2002), http://octopus.bch.cuhk.edu.hk/fun7/english/primary-EatingOut-receipt.shtml.

**bone girl**: Xocat Forum (June 29, 2009), http://forum.timway.com/f/viewthread.php?action=printable&tid=272726.

**bor law yau**: Choy So Yuk, *Letter to Hong Kong*, Radio Television Hong Kong, Radio 3 (December 9, 2007).

**B quality**: Personal statement made by a hawker of counterfeit goods.

**B shares**: Van Hoa Tran (ed.), *China's Trade and Investment After the Asia Crisis* (Cheltenham, UK: Edward Elgar, 2000), p. 81.

**bubble tea**: The Hong Kong General Chamber of Commerce, "Member's profile: Saint's Alp Teahouse" (2010), http://www.chamber.org.

hk/info/member_a_week/member_profile.
asp?id=53.

**Buddha's Birthday**: Michael Ingham, *Hong Kong: A Cultural History* (New York: Oxford University Press, 2007), p. 195.

**cagehome**: Nemo Wu Xuling, "The Young Reporter online: Life in the cage," http://www.hkbu. edu.hk/~tyrej/37_2/37_2_n05.htm.

**cageman**, also **cagepeople**: Internet Movie Database, *Lung Min* (1992), http://www. imdb.com/title/tt0107461/.

**candareen**: T. W. Pearce and J. H. Stewart-Lockhart, "Enigmatic parallelisms of the Canton dialect." *The China Review, or Notes and Queries on the Far East*, 15(3) (1886): 42.

**Cantonese**: ❶ galaxylink.co.hk, "Cantonese recipes" (n.d.), http://www.galaxylink.com. hk/~john/food/cooking/canton/canton.htm. ❷ Cantonese.hk (August 14, 2010), http:// cantonese.hk/wp/.

**Canto-pop**: Robert Storey, *Hong Kong, Macau and Canton* (Hawthorn, Victoria: Lonely Planet, 1992), p. 26.

**caput school**: Immanuel Lutheran College, "School history" (August 26, 2003), http://www.ilc. edu.hk/school_info/school_history.htm.

**carabao**: Bien Perez, "Expats keen for scoop of Filipino ice cream." *The Standard* (May 23, 1995).

**category I, IIA, IIB, III**: K. C. Kwong, Secretary for Information Technology and Broadcasting, "Film censorship guidelines for censors" (December 3, 1999), http://www.tela.gov.hk/ english/doc/forms/filmcensorship.pdf.

**catty**: Hong Kong Legal Information Institute. Hong Kong Ordinances, "Weights and measures ordinances: Schedule 1 (enacted 1987)" (n.d.), http://www.hklii.org/hk/legis/en/ord/68/sch1.html.

**CBC**: discuss.com.hk, userid: dancingirl (May 9, 2006), http://www10.discuss.com.hk/archiver/?tid-840227-page-18.html.

**celestial**: Thomas R. Dewar, *A Ramble Round the Globe* (London: Chatto and Windus, 1894), p. 211.

**Celestial Empire/Kingdom**: ❶ Solomon Bard, "Tea and opium." *Journal of the Hong Kong Branch of the Royal Asiatic Society*, 40(2) (2000): 6, http://sunzi1.lib.hku.hk/hkjo/view/44/4400860.pdf.

**Central**: Donald Asprey, "Police gear up for holiday crowd." *The Standard* (December 22, 2006).

**century egg**: Yahoo, userid: Mashini (2010), http://knowledge.yahoo.com.hk/question/?qid=7006112700013&others=1.

**char chaan teng**, also **cha chaan teng**, **cha chaan tang**: ❶ Choy So Yuk, Letter to Hong Kong, Radio Television Hong Kong, Radio 3 (December 9, 2007). ❷ 12hk.com, "The unofficial guide to Hong Kong tea restaurants ('cha chaan tang')" (2009), http://www.12hk.com/food/TeaRestaurant.html.

**char siu**, also **char siew**, **cha siu**, **char su**, and **char siu bau**, **char su bau**, **cha siu bau**, **char siew bau**: ❶ The International Asian Studies Programme (IASP) Newsletter 2006–07, Office of Academic Links, The Chinese

University of Hong Kong (Issue December 5, 2006), http://www.cuhk.edu.hk/oal/newsletter/0607/Issue5_Dec_2006/Issue5.htm. ❷ 12hk.com, "Food in Hong Kong" (2004–10), http://www.12hk.com/food/hk_food.shtml.

**chau**: *Hong Kong Guidebook: Ap Lei Chau, Cheung Chau and Peng Chau* (Hong Kong: Universal Publication, 2000), pp. 87, 26, 133.

**chee-saw**: Nury Vittachi, *Asian Values* (Hong Kong: Chameleon Press, 1996), p. 103.

**chek**: Hong Kong Legal Information Institute. Hong Kong Ordinances, "Weights and measures ordinances: Schedule 1 (enacted 1987)" (n.d.), http://www.hklii.org/hk/legis/en/ord/68/sch1.html.

**cheong fun**: Food wrapper, Amoy Food Ltd.

**cheongsam**: "Water colors." *The Standard* (November 26, 2005), http://www.thestandard.com.hk/weekend_news_detail.asp?pp_cat=30&art_id=6452&sid=5601173&con_type=3&d_str=20051126.

**Cheung Chau Bun Festival**: Michael Ingham, *Hong Kong: A Cultural History* (New York: Oxford University Press, 2007), p. 23.

**chick**, **chicken**: The Associated Press, "Hong Kong police arrest 24 suspected male prostitutes" (2005), http://english.sina.com/taiwan_hk/1/2005/0204/20567.html.

**chicken-worm**: *Ironside 426* DVD (Hong Kong version), product description.

**China doll**: "Beauty in Liu of brains." *The Standard* (June 10, 2006), http://www.thestandard.com.hk/weekend_news_detail.

asp?pp_cat=41&art_id=20477&sid=7607928 &con_type=1&d_str=20060610.

**Chinese**: Hong Kong Baptist University, "Faculty of Arts: Language Courses" (2004), http://arts.hkbu.edu.hk/lang.asp.

**Chinese parsley**: Hong Kong Asiaxpat.com, "Hong Kong Advice Forums: Recipes and cooking" (2008), http://hongkong.asiaxpat.com/forums/recipes-cooking/threads/115583/continental-parsley-(in-large-quantities)?/.

**Chinese Valentine's Day**: Jody Marshall, *English Speaking Student's Book II* (Beijing: Qinghua Daxue Chubanshe, 2006), p. 60.

**Chinglish**: Larry Feign, *Hongkongitis: Reports from the Wackiest Place on Earth* (Hong Kong: Chameleon Press, 2007), p. 137.

**Ching Ming**: China Droll, "Cecilie: Nature worshippers" (April 5, 2009), http://www.chinadroll.com/?p=849.

**Chippies**, also **Chuppies**: ❶ Richard Sterling, Elizabeth Chong, and Lushan Charles Qin, *World Food Hong Kong (Lonely Planet World Food Guides)* (Footscray, Victoria: Lonely Planet Publications, 2001), p. 157. ❷ Wu Zhong, "Chuppie culture." *The Standard* (November 22, 2004).

**chit**: The Government of the Hong Kong Special Administrative Region, "Environmental performance report," Chapter 5, "Sustainability at EPD: Economic impacts" (2006), http://www.epd.gov.hk/epd/misc/er/er2006/english/ch_5.html.

**chit-fund**: The Government of the Hong Kong Special Administrative Region, "Sources of finance for civil servants" (2010), p. 6, http://www.csb.gov.hk/english/publication/files/efin.pdf.

**choi sum**, also **choy sum**: ❶ Rosemary Sayer, "Gordon Wu: The man who turned the lights on" (n.d.), http://www.cosmosbooks.com.hk/topic_a/page_0.asp?topic=2&bookid=309980. ❷ Dung Kai Cheung, "The Young Shen Nong." In Eva Hung (ed.), *Hong Kong Stories: Old Themes New Voices* (Hong Kong: Research Centre for Translation, the Chinese University of Hong Kong, 1999), p. 124.

**chop**: ❶ Principal: Downloads/Admin Forms (n.d.), http://www.principal.com.hk/allweb/english/001_adminform.asp. ❷ José Maria Braga, Hong Kong Business Symposium (Hong Kong, 1957), p. 437. ❸ Alain Le Pichon, *China Trade and Empire: Jardine, Matheson & Co. and the Origins of British Rule in Hong Kong, 1827–1843* (New York: Oxford University Press, 2006), p. 476.

**chop-boat**: Katharine Hillard (ed.), "A Letter." In *My Mother's Journal. A Young Lady's Diary of Five Years Spent in Manila, Macao, and the Cape of Good Hope from 1829–1834* (Boston: George H. Ellis, 1900), p. 82.

**chop-chop**: Larry Feign, *Banned in Hong Kong* (Hong Kong: Hambalan, 1995), p. 57.

**chop-house**: William Dallas Bernard (ed.), from *Notes of Commander W. H. Hall: Narrative of the Voyages and Services of the Nemesis from 1840 to 1843* (London : Henry Colburn, 1844), p. 383.

**chopped dollar**: G. J. Younghusband, *On Short*

*Leave to Japan* (London: S. Low, Marston and Co. Ltd., 1894), p. 46.

**chop suey**: ❶ Xu Xi, *The Unwalled City* (Hong Kong: Chameleon Press, 2001), p. 251. ❷ Rupert Chan, "Appreciation of the art of opera: Turandot's homecoming." LCSD-cultural presentations section (2005), http://www. lcsd.gov.hk/CE/CulturalService/Programme/ en/music/jul05/threesong.html. ❸ Shu-fan Li, *Hong Kong Surgeon* (Hong Kong: Li Shu Fan Medical Foundation, 1964), p. 168.

**chow-chow**: ❶ J. Nacken, "Chinese street-cries in Hongkong." *Journal of the Hong Kong Branch of the Royal Asiatic Society* 8 (1968): 128–134, 132. ❷ William C. Hunter, *The 'Fan Kwae' at Canton Before Treaty Days, 1825–1844* (Shanghai: Kelly and Walsh, 1911), p. 62.

**chow fan**: *Eat and Travel Weekly* (March 21, 2003).

**chow mein**: see **chow fan**.

**Christian**: Tim Hamlett, "The Young Reporter Style Book" (2004), p. 27, http://journalism.hkbu. edu.hk/doc/054_TYR_style2004.pdf.

**chuk kam**: Hong Kong Legal Information Institute. "Trade descriptions (marking) (gold and gold alloy) order: Schedule 1 standards of fineness," June 30, 1997, http://www.hklii. org/hk/legis/en/reg/362A.txt.

**Chung Yeung Festival**: Solomon Bard, *Voices from the Past: Hong Kong, 1842–1918* (Hong Kong: Hong Kong University Press, 2002), p. 306.

**circulating libraries**: Anonymous, "Walks about Canton: Extracts from a private journal."

*The Chinese Repository*, IV, 1835–36 (1836), p. 190.

**civet cat**: Yiu Wing Kam et al., "Antibodies against trimeric S glycoprotein protect hamsters against SARS-CoV challenge despite their capacity to mediate Fc RII-dependent entry into B cells in vitro." *Vaccine*, 25 (2007): 729–740, 737.

**Co-hong**: Wei Peh T'i, "Juan Yuan's management of Sino-British relations in Canton 1817–1826." *Journal of the Hong Kong Branch of the Royal Asiatic Society* 21 (1981): 146, http://sunzi1.lib.hku.hk/hkjo/view/44/4401476.pdf.

**compensated dating**: Nickkita Lau, "Teen girls sell sex via the internet." *The Standard* (October 15, 2007), http://www.thestandard.com.hk/news_print.asp?art_id=55133&sid=15810773.

**comprador**, also **compradore**: ❶ Ng Lun Ngai-Ha, "The Hong Kong origins of Dr. Sun Yat-Sen's address to Li Hung-Chang." *Journal of the Hong Kong Branch of the Royal Asiatic Society*, 21 (1981): 168–178, 172. ❷ Irene Cheng, *Clara Ho Tung, A Hong Kong Lady: Her Family and Her Times* (Hong Kong: The Chinese University of Hong Kong, 1976), p. 23.

**compradore account**: May Holdsworth (with additional text by Caroline Courtauld), *Foreign Devils: Expatriates in Hong Kong* (Oxford: Oxford University Press, 2002), p. 23.

**compradorship**: Irene Cheng, *Clara Ho Tung, A Hong Kong Lady: Her Family and Her Times*

(Hong Kong: The Chinese University of
Hong Kong, 1976), p. 8.

**Confucius, Birthday of**: The Hong Kong Government
of the Special Administrative Region,
Information Services Department, *Hong Kong
2001* (Hong Kong: Information Services
Department, the Government of the Hong
Kong Special Administrative Region, 2001),
p. 394.

**congee**: Interesting information (n.d.), http://
www.oceanempire.com.hk/web_develop/
inform(e).htm.

**coolie**, also **cooly**: ❶ Fook Loong (HK) Ltd., "Current
use: Terms and conditions of sale" (n.d.),
http://www.flhk.com.hk/pdf_files/FL-TERM-
rev1.PDF. ❷ Archaic use: Urban Council,
*City of Victoria* (Hong Kong: Urban Council,
1994), p. 63. ❸ D. G. Rites performed for the
dead. *The China Review*, 10(2) (1881): 145–
146, 146.

**copy**: eBay, "NEW SEALED *Prison Break* Season
ONE 1 2006 DVD BOX SET" (n.d.), http://
cgi.ebay.com.hk/ws/eBayISAPI.dll?ViewIte
m&item=120099315401.

**crossed cheque**: Mouth and Foot Painting Artists
Limited invoice.

**cross-strait**: The Secretary for Constitutional Affairs'
speech at the lunch for speakers of CS forum
on cross-strait peace and development, press
release (June 15, 2006), http://www.info.gov.
hk/gia/general/200606/15/P200606150289.
htm.

**cumshaw**: Ernest John Eitel, *Europe in China: The
History of Hongkong from the Beginning*

*to the Year 1882* (London: Luzac and Co., 1895), p. 20.

**D**: Hong Kong Television and Entertainment Licensing Authority, *Glossary of Undesirable Expressions* (Hong Kong: Hong Kong Television and Entertainment Licensing Authority, 1983).

**dai jap hai**: maximus, "HySaN Posse TA Cafe" (Part III) (2009), http://www4.uwants.com/archiver/?tid-8541476-page-96.html.

**dai pai dong**: Robert Storey, *Hong Kong, Macau and Canton* (Hawthorn, Victoria: Lonely Planet, 1992), p. 72.

**dan tat**, also **daan tat**: *Hong Kong Magazine*, One Stop Shop (November 26, 2004), http://www.specialisthk.com/sphk/en/html/.../what_dining_cuisine.html.

**dim sum**: Xu Xi, *The Unwalled City* (Hong Kong: Chameleon Press, 2001), p. 79.

**dim sum house**: Clement Poon, "Opera not just for aristocrats." *The Standard* (October 20, 1994), http://www.thestandard.com.hk/archive_news_detail.asp?pp_cat=&art_id=2085&sid=&con_type=1&archive_d_str=19941020.

**do-jeh**: Leanne Nicholls, *Newsletter*, 1 (2002), http://www.ccohk.com/Newsletters/issue1.html.

**domestic helper**: Joseph Bosco, "The MacDonald's Snoopy craze in Hong Kong." In Gordon Mathews and Tai-Lok Lui (eds.), *Consuming Hong Kong* (Hong Kong: Hong Kong University Press, 2001), p. 264.

**Double Tenth:** ❶ Maggie Keswick (ed.), *The Thistle and The Jade: A Celebration of 175 Years* *of Jardine Matheson* (London: Frances Lincoln, 2008), p. 304. ❷ K. C. Wong and K. K. Yuen (eds., adapted by T. K. Chung), "Essays: Nanking Period" (1982), http://www.thecorner.org/hist/essays/china/nanking_period.htm.

**doubling-down**: The Government of the Hong Kong Special Administrative Region, "Legislative Council Panel on Public Service: Review of acting appointment system" (1999), p. 2, http://www.legco.gov.hk/yr99-00/english/panels/ps/papers/a632e.pdf.

**doubling-sideways**: The Government of the Hong Kong Special Administrative Region, General Revenue Account, Government Secretariat, Civil Service Bureau, Audit Commission, "Administration of allowances in the civil service" (1999), http://www.aud.gov.hk/pdf_e/e33ch08.pdf.

**doubling-up**: See **doubling-sideways**.

**dou fu fa**: J. S. Lam, "Crooks more slapstick than stickup." *The Standard* (2010), p. 14, http://www.thestandard.com.hk/news_detail.asp?we_cat=5&art_id=102388&sid=29417555&con_type=1&d_str=20100901&fc=7.

**drunken chicken**: *Free China Review*, 43(7–12) (1993): 40.

**elderlies**: M. H. Chan, Y. C. Lee, N. S. Ng, "Usefulness of microbiological investigations in the management of infections in the elderlies." *Journal of the Hong Kong Geriatric Society*, l (1) (1993): 32–34, 32. [Note: From Geriatric Unit, Princess Margaret Hospital.]

**estate**: ❶ Lawrence Wai-Chung Lai with Ki Fong, *Town Planning Practice: Context, Procedures and Statistics for Hong Kong* (Hong Kong: Hong Kong University Press, 2000), p. 48. ❷ T. N. Chiu and C. L. So (eds.), *A Geography of Hong Kong* (Hong Kong: Oxford University Press, 1983), p. 185.

**face**: The University of Hong Kong, Centre for Suicide Research and Prevention, "The psychological autopsy study of suicides in Hong Kong" (n.d.), p. 26, http://csrp.hku.hk/files/589_2754_471.pdf.

**Falun Gong**: Glenn Schloss, "The strange world of Li Hongzhi." *The Hong Kong Standard* (July 25, 1999).

**fan** (1): aboutdishes.com, "Chinese dining etiquette" (n.d.), http://www.aboutdishes.com/art_of_eating/oriental/chinese.html.

**fan** (2): See **catty**.

**fan** (3): See **chek**.

**fan gwei(lo)**, also **fanqui**, **fan kwai**, **fan-kwei**: ❶ May Holdsworth (with additional text by Caroline Courtauld), *Foreign Devils: Expatriates in Hong Kong* (Oxford: Oxford University Press, 2002), p. xiii. ❷ May Holdsworth, *Foreign Devils* (2002), p. 47. ❸ Osmond Tiffany, *The Canton Chinese or the American's Sojourn in the Celestial Empire* (Boston and Cambridge: James Munroe and Company, 1849), p. 26. ❹ Wong Man-kong, "The use of Sinology in the nineteenth century: Two perspectives revealed in the history of Hong Kong." In Lee Pui-tak (ed.), *Colonial Hong Kong and Modern China:*

*Interaction and Reintegration*, (Hong Kong: Hong Kong University Press, 2005), p. 149. ❺ Albert Smith, *To China and Back: Being a Diary Kept, Out and Home* (1859), p. 47.

**fan tan**: ❶ The Government of the Hong Kong Special Administrative Region, Home Affairs Bureau, "A study of Hong Kong people's participation in gambling activities" (2005), p. 43, http://www.hab.gov.hk/file_manager/en/documents/publications_and_press_releases/20051214gambling_hkureport_e.pdf. ❷ Roy Rowan, *Chasing the Dragon: A Veteran Journalist's Firsthand Account of the 1946–9 Chinese Revolution* (Guilford, CT: Lyons Press, 2008), p. 172.

**fat choi**, also **fat choy**: ❶ "Don't mess with black moss." *The Student Standard* (February 14, 2007), http://student.thestandard.com.hk/liberal/PDF/s/file_20070215172854070554.pdf. ❷ James O'Reilly, Larry Habegger, Sean O'Reilly (eds.), *Traveler's Tales Hong Kong: Including Macau and Southern China* (San Francisco: Travelers' Tales, 1996), p. 143.

**fen**: Anthony Walker, Denis Levett, and Roger Flanagan, *China: Building for Joint Ventures*, second edition (Hong Kong: Hong Kong University Press, 1998), p. 6.

**FILTH**: Muhammad Cohen, *Hong Kong on Air* (Hong Kong: Blacksmith Books, 2007), p. 21.

**foki**: ❶ Deputy District Judge Abu B. bin Wahab, "Judgement in the district court of the Hong Kong SAR Employees' Compensation case no. 1242 of 2005" (June 15, 2007). ❷ Vivienne Poy, *Building Bridges: The Life* and *Times of Richard Charles Lee: Hong Kong, 1905–1983* (Scarborough, Ont.: Calyan Publishing Ltd., 1998), p. 24.

**foreign mud**: Economist.com, "Cities Guide, Hong Kong" (n.d.), http://www.economist.com.hk/cities/findStory.cfm?city_id=HK&folder=Facts-History.

**fruit money**: Nicole Newendorp, *Uneasy Reunions: Immigration, Citizenship, and Family Life in Post-1997 Hong Kong* (Stanford: Stanford University Press, 2008), p. 61.

**fu mo kwun**: James Hayes, "The New Territories twenty years ago: From the notebooks of a District Officer." *Hong Kong Journal of Public Administration*, 2(1) (1980): 60–70, 62.

**fung shui**: Nury Vittachi, *Reliable Sauce: The Secret Diaries of Lai See* (Hong Kong: Pacific Century Books, 1991), p. 136.

**gai lan**: OpenRice.com, "Under bridge spicy crab" (2010), http://www.openrice.com/english/restaurant/commentdetail.htm?commentid=2056347.

**gaylo**: Lenny's guest book (n.d.), http://www.glink.net.hk/~lchen/guestbook.html.

**gei wai**: Florence Ng, "Road Test: Mai Po nature reserve." *South China Morning Post*, Sunday Review Section (October 6, 2002), p. 9.

**General Kwan**, also **Gwan Yu**: ebay.com.hk, "Antique Chinese General Kwan Snuff Bottle: Early 1800s" (August 2008), http://cgi.ebay.com.hk/ws/eBayISAPI.dll?ViewItem&item=150070248565.

**ghost**: *South China Morning Post* (August 28, 2003), p. 13.

**godown**: Urban Council, *City of Victoria* (Hong Kong: Urban Council, 1994), p. 63.

**golden lily feet**: Constance Gordon Cumming, *Wanderings in China* (1886), p. 48.

**Golden Mountain**: ❶ David T. K. Wong, "Red, amber, green." In Xu Xi and Mike Ingham (eds.), *City Voices: Hong Kong Writing in English, 1945 to the Present* (Hong Kong: Hong Kong University Press, 2003), p. 112. ❷ Michael Ingham, *Hong Kong: A Cultural History* (New York: Oxford University Press, 2007), p. 217.

**golden rice bowl**: Diana Lee, "Pay rise boosts turnout for police recruitment." *The Standard* (July 9, 2007).

**grand chop**: Alain Le Pichon, *China Trade and Empire: Jardine, Matheson & Co. and the Origins of British Rule in Hong Kong, 1827–1843* (New York: Oxford University Press, 2006), p. 15.

**green hat**: AsiaXPAT.com (2007), http://hongkong.asiaxpat.com/forums/marriage-relationships/threads/101359/what-do-i-do/.

**griffin**: ❶ Griffin trials at Sha Tin (September 26, 2001), http://www.hkjc.com/english/news/news_200109261071.htm. ❷ Marjorie Topley (ed.), *Hong Kong: The Interaction of Traditions and Life in the Towns* (Hong Kong: Hong Kong Branch of the Royal Asiatic Society), p. 62.

**grinding bean curd**: Wayne R. Dynes and Stephen Donaldson (eds.), *Asian Homosexuality* (New York: Garland Pub, 1992), p. 101.

**guanxi**: Dennis Bloodworth and Liang Ching Ping, *I Married a Barbarian* (Singapore: Times Books International, 2000), p. 171.

**gwai jai**: Beautyexchange.com.hk, userid: Molko (May 18, 2008), http://www.beautyexchange. com.hk/revamp/forums/read.php?4,408 1040.

**gwai mui**: Live Journal Community, Yung Poo Ci (2005), http://community.livejournal.com/ yung_poo_ci/930.html.

**gwaipoh**, also **gweipo**, **gwaipo**, **gwaipor**: ❶ Larry Feign, *Execute Yourself Tonite* (Hong Kong: Hambalan Press, 1993), p. 58. ❷ The Dark Side, "The Other Side of Hong Kong" (June 18, 2010), http://thedarkside.hk/2010/06/18/ china-worldcup-bodypaint-chicks/ ❸ Xu Xi, *The Unwalled City* (Hong Kong: Chameleon Press, 2001), p. 74. ❹ Nury Vittachi, *The Hong Kong Joke Book* (Hong Kong: Chameleon Press, 1995), p. 149.

**gweilo**, also **gwailo**: ❶ *South China Morning Post*, Features (December 13, 2002), p. 1. ❷ Nury Vittachi, *Travellers' Tales* (Hong Kong: Far East Economic Review Publications, 1994), p. 127.

**haam daan**: Richard Sterling, Elizabeth Chong, and Lushan Charles Qin, *World Food Hong Kong (Lonely Planet World Food Guides)* (Footscray, Victoria: Lonely Planet Publications, 2001), p. 56.

**hairy gourd**: Diana Yue Xi Xi, *Flying Carpet: A Tale of Fertillia* (Hong Kong: Hong Kong University Press, 2000), p. 267.

**hak gwai**, also **hak gwei**: ❶ Ravina Shamdasani, "Nigerian woman claims police bias over fight." *South China Morning Post*, City Section (June 27, 2003), p. C4. ❷ Chip Tsao, "On living with Obama." *HK Magazine* (November 21, 2008), p. 11.

**Hakka**: Sidney Cheung, "Hakka restaurants: A study of the consumption of food in post-war Hong Kong society." In David Y. H. Wu and Tan Chee-beng (eds.), *Changing Chinese Foodways in Asia* (Hong Kong: Chinese University Press, 2001), p. 81.

**hand tail**: Smartclub.com.hk (July 24, 2005), http://smartclub.com.hk/forum/viewtopic. php?t=4118&start=0&sid=e1b5e3d6217d185 1a159eb50694f2371.

**har gow**, also **har gau**, **ha gao**, **har kow**: ❶ Steve Temkin, "Some classy little bites." *The Standard* (April 30, 1995), http://www. thestandard.com.hk/archive_news_detail. asp?pp_cat=&art_id=9371&sid=&con_type= 1&archive_d_str=19950430. ❷ *South China Morning Post*, The Post Magazine (September 15, 2002), p. 57. ❸ Nigel Cameron, *Hong Kong: The Cultured Pearl* (Hong Kong: Oxford University Press, 1978), p. 210. ❹ Rosa Lo San Ross, *365 Ways to Cook Chinese* (New York: Harper Collins, 1994), p. 193.

**hasma soup**: Richard Sterling, Elizabeth Chong, and Lushan Charles Qin, *World Food Hong Kong (Lonely Planet World Food Guides)* (Footscray, Victoria: Lonely Planet Publications, 2001), p. 119.

**haw fun**: Richard Sterling, Elizabeth Chong, and Lushan Charles Qin, *World Food Hong Kong (Lonely Planet World Food*

*Guides)* (Footscray, Victoria: Lonely Planet Publications, 2001), p. 37.

**hell**: Chen Yaoting, "The Emperor of the Fengdu Hell" (n.d.), http://eng.taoism.org.hk/daoist-beliefs/immortals-immortalism/pg2-4-7-1.htm.

**heung cheung**: Austin Coates, *Myself a Mandarin: Memoirs of a Special Magistrate* (Omaha, NE: The John Day Company, 1969), p. 70.

**heung ha**: Nury Vittachi, *Asian Values* (Hong Kong: Chameleon Press, 1996), p. 53.

**hill fire**: Anthony Sweeting, *Education in Hong Kong, 1941 to 2001: Visions and Revisions* (Hong Kong: Hong Kong University Press, 1996), p. 445.

**hit airplane**: 141hongkong.com, "SEX141" (October 9, 2007), http://141hongkong.com/forum/archiver/?tid-67297.html.

**HKSAR Establishment Day**: Yiu-chung Wong (ed.), *One Country, Two Systems' in Crisis: Hong Kong's Transformation Since the Handover* (Lanham: Lexington Books, 2004), p. 53.

**hoisin sauce**: Richard Sterling, Elizabeth Chong, and Lushan Charles Qin, *World Food Hong Kong (Lonely Planet World Food Guides)* (Footscray, Victoria: Lonely Planet Publications, 2001), p. 57.

**hong**: Meng Xiaoshu, "Hongs supporting Patten's political reforms paid price in lost deals and isolation by China." *The Standard* (May 25, 1996), http://www.thestandard.com.hk/archive_news_detail.asp?pp_cat=&art_id=16069&sid=&con_type=1&archive_d_str=19960525.

**hong-boat**: Society for the Propagation of the Gospel in Foreign Parts, "Work in the Colonies" (1865), p. 247.

**Hongcouver**: Nury Vittachi, *Reliable Sauce: The Secret Diaries of Lai See* (Hong Kong: Pacific Century Books, 1991), p. 41.

**Hongkie** (1): Tomorrow, "Hongkies suck" (July 5, 2007), http://tomorrow.sg/archives/2007/07/02/hongkies_suck.html.

**Hongkie** (2): Muhammad Cohen, *Hong Kong on Air* (Hong Kong: Blacksmith Books, 2007), p. 143.

**Hongkonger**, also **Hong Konger**: ❶ The Government of the Hong Kong Special Administrative Region, "The Secretary for Education and Manpower's (SEM) speech at Hong Kong Outstanding Students' Association—Youth Summit 2005" (2005), http://www.info.gov.hk/gia/general/200504/02/04020134.htm. ❷ see **tong sui**.

**Hongkongeress**: Susanna Hoe, *The Private Life of Old Hong Kong: Western Women in the British Colony 1841–1941* (Hong Kong: Oxford University Press, 1991), p. 182.

**Hong Kong Flu**: Ray Cheung, "How HKU scientists helped save Hong Kong's people" (2001), http://www.hku.hk/daao/newsletter/web_0103/chicken.doc.

**Hong Kong foot**: The Government of the Hong Kong Special Administrative Region, Elderly Health Services, Department of Health (2006), http://www.info.gov.hk/elderly/english/healthinfo/selfhelptips/skincare.htm.

**Honkers**: Donald Tsang, "Hong Kong: Looking towards the future" (speech) (August 25, 1997), http://www.info.gov.hk/isd/speech/fs97825.htm.

**house-coolie**: Oliver G. Ready, *Life and Sport in China* (London: Chapman and Hall, 1904), p. 37.

**H share**: John Dodsworth and Dubravko Mihaljek, *Hong Kong, China: Growth, Structural Change, and Economic Stability During the Transition* (Washington, DC: International Monetary Fund, 1997), p. 43.

**hui**, also **hoey**: ❶ Victor Mok and Joseph Wu, "Yi Hui and 'Yin Hui': An introductory analysis." *Chung Chi Journal*, 11(1) (1972): 126–137, 126. ❷ John Coming, *Bright Celestials: The Chinaman at Home and Abroad* (1894), p. 184.

**II**: The Government of the Hong Kong Special Administrative Region, "Joint Guangdong-HK meeting on boundary security and anti-II measures" (2001), http://www.info.gov.hk/gia/general/200107/24/0724320.htm.

**iron rice bowl**: Patricia Fosh, Andy W. Chan, Wilson W. S. Chow, Ed Snape, and Robert Westwood (eds.), *Hong Kong Management and Labour: Change and Continuity* (New York: Routledge, 1999), p. 140.

**Jardine Johnnies**: Gren Manuel, "Just add cash for instant unqualified success." *The Standard* (May 10, 1995), http://www.thestandard.com.hk/archive_news_detail.asp?pp_cat=&art_id=10174&sid=&con_type=1&archive_d_str=19950510.

**jetso**: Dah Sing Bank Limited, "Personal: Credit Card: Jetso Corner, Jetso Spending Offer," (2010), http://www.dahsing.com/en/html/credit_card/jetso/jetsospendingoffer.html.

**jiao**: International Conference on Asian Green Electronics: Design for Manufacturability and Reliability website (2005), http://www.ee.cityu.edu.hk/~agec/travel.htm.

**John Company**: The University of Hong Kong, "HISY1006: The West in the 19th Century" (n.d.), http://hkuhist2.hku.hk/history/firstyear/governorsmacau.htm.

**jo san**, also **jo sun**: ❶ The Tang Family guestbook (n.d..), www.tangfamily.com.hk/guest.php?page=4. ❷ Signature Homes anniversary celebration (n.d.), http://www.signaturehomes.com.hk/script/en/anniversary/3rd_a.html.

**joss**: Frank Sanello, *The Opium Wars: The Addiction of One Empire and the Corruption of Another* (Naperville, IL: Sourcebooks, 2004), p. 127.

**joss house**: The University of Hong Kong, "The social history of Hong Kong" (n.d.), http://www.hku.hk/hkcsp/ccex/text/studyguide/hkhist/ch1_6s.htm.

**joss paper**: ❶ J. W. Hayes, "A ceremony to propitiate the gods at Tong Fuk, Lantau, 1958." *Journal of the Royal Asiatic Society Hong Kong Branch* 5 (1965): 122–124, 124. ❷ Gillian Bickley, Bickley Verner, and Coghlan Christopher (eds.), *A Magistrate's Court in 19th Century Hong Kong: Court in Time* (Hong Kong: Proverse Hong Kong, 2005), p. 78.

**joss stick**: Judy Ling and Anne Smith, *My Pals Are Here*, "Take a Break" (Singapore, Marshall Cavendish Education 2005). [Note: This is a children's book published in Singapore, but found in Hong Kong schools.]

**juk**, also **jook**: ❶ Tim Hamlett, "The Young Reporter Style Book" (2004), p. 52, http://journalism.hkbu.edu.hk/doc/ 054_TYR_style2004.pdf. ❷ Rosa Lo San Ross, *365 Ways to Cook Chinese* (New York: Harper Collins, 1994), p. 140.

**July 1st**, also **July First**: ❶ Helen F. Siu, "Positioning 'Hongkongers' and 'new immigrants.'" In Helen F. Siu and Agnes S. Ku (ed.), *Hong Kong Mobile: Making a Global Population* (Hong Kong: Hong Kong University Press, 2008), p. 146. ❷ Radio Television Hong Kong, "Protest against consultation delay" (January 16, 2009), http://www.rthk.org. hk/rthk/news/englishnews/20090116/ news_20090116_56_552897.htm.

**junk**, also **djunk**: Harold Ingrams, *Hong Kong* (London: Her Majesty's Stationery Office, 1952), p. 39.

**ju yug bao**: Richard Sterling, Elizabeth Chong, and Lushan Charles Qin, *World Food Hong Kong (Lonely Planet World Food Guides)* (Footscray, Victoria: Lonely Planet Publications, 2001), p. 201.

**kaido (ferry)**, also **kaito**: ❶ The Government of the Hong Kong Special Administrative Region, Transport Department, "Termination of 'Kaito' Ferry service" (2009), www.td.gov. hk/en/traffic_notices/index_t_id_17703.

html. ❷ Hong Kong Tourism Board, "Peng Chau Island: Hong Kong Island" (2010), www.secure.discoverhongkong.com/eng/attractions/green-pengchau.html.

**kaifong**: ❶ F. J. Shulman, *Doctoral Dissertations on Hong Kong, 1900–1997: An Annotated Bibliography* (Hong Kong: Hong Kong University Press, 2001), p. 24. ❷ S. Lam, "Officers relied on their whistle and wits." *The Standard* (July 5, 2010), p. 17, http://www.thestandard.com.hk/news_detail.asp?pp_cat=15&art_id=100050&sid=28750105&con_type=1&d_str=20100705.

**Kai Tak rules**: Hong Kong Cricket Club, "Message from Chris and Taffy …" (2009), http://www.hkcc.org/section5_8.html.

**kan**: September Hong Kong Jewellery and Gem Fair, "Press release" (2008), http://exhibitions.jewellerynetasia.com/exhibitions/release.asp?sectid=5&subid=8&siteid=5&lang=1&pressid=232.

**kang**: Altfield gallery online (n.d.), http://www.altfield.com.hk/Exhibitions.html.

**kang kong**: My Wok Life, "Seafood dinner tour in Lamma Island, Hong Kong" (2009), http://www.mywoklife.com/2009/03/seafood-dinner-tour-in-lamma-island.html.

**kit fat**: Austin Coates, *Myself a Mandarin: Memoirs of a Special Magistrate* (Omaha, NE: The John Day Company, 1969), p. 28.

**Kowloon**: ❶ Wong Kwok-keung, "Welcome message from the chairman of the Kowloon City District Council" (2010), www.districtcouncils.gov.hk/klc/english/

welcome.htm. ❷ Annie Roo, R. Jagtenberg, and Robert W. Jagtenberg: *Yearbook Law and Legal Practice in East Asia 1995* (The Hague: Kluwer Law International, 1995), p. 96.

**Kowloon City**: ❶ Rowena Y. F. Kwok, Joan Y. H. Leung, and Ian Scott (eds.), *Votes without Power: The Hong Kong Legislative Council Elections* (Hong Kong: Hong Kong University Press, 1992), p. 39. ❷ Roger Nissim, *Land Administration and Practice in Hong Kong* (Hong Kong: Hong Kong University Press, 2008), p. 21.

**Kowloon Walled City**: Kowloon City District Council, "Overview of Kowloon City" (2010), www.districtcouncils.gov.hk/klc_d/english/dchighlights.htm.

**kowtow**: ❶ Richard R. Wertz, "The Cultural heritage of China: Food and drink: Tea: Tea Cultures" (1998–2009), http://www.ibiblio.org/chineseculture/contents/food/p-food-c03s03.html. ❷ Yuen-Fong Woon, "Social organization and ceremonial life of two multi-surname villages in Hoi-p'ing County, South China, 1911–1949." *Journal of the Hong Kong Branch of the Royal Asiatic Society*, 17 (1977): 101–111, p. 103. ❸ "Seoul warning to US hawks." *The Standard* (January 26, 2006), http://www.thestandard.com.hk/news_detail.asp?we_cat=6&art_id=10800&sid=6387249&con_type=1&d_str=20060126.

**kuk**: Po Leung Kuk, "Founding of Po Leung Kuk" (2010), http://www.poleungkuk.org.hk/plk/admin/Data/PageContentPage/ContentPage/20060804114558/e_index.html.

**kung hei fat choy**: Joseph Yam, chief executive, Hong Kong Monetary Authority, "Viewpoint: Kung Hei Fat Choy" (2000), http://www.info.gov.hk/hkma/eng/viewpt/20000203e.htm.

**kung-so**: Urban Council, *City of Victoria* (Hong Kong: Urban Council, 1994), p. 55.

**Kwun Tong**: Chan Chung-bun, chairman, Kwun Tong District Council, "Welcome speech" (2010), http://www.districtcouncils.gov.hk/kt/text_english/welcome.htm.

**lai cha**: Nury Vittachi, *The Shanghai Union of Industrial Mystics* (Edinburgh: Polygon, 2007), p. 75.

**lai see**: ❶ Carol Chung, "More lucky money to go around." *The Standard* (February 13, 2007), http://www.thestandard.com.hk/news_detail.asp?we_cat=4&art_id=38205&sid=12188810&con_type=1&d_str=20070213. ❷ Hysan Development Company Limited, Human Resources Department, "Code of ethics" (2005), Chapter 9 personal benefits, http://www.hysan.com.hk/eng/news/annual_report/Appendix%202_e.doc.

**lakh**: njboxnorth.dekarabaw.com, "The Manchester Blog Awards explained and Manchester sewer bills headed for big increase" (2007), http://njboxnorth.dekarabaw.com.

**laliloon**: Major W. H. Poyntz, *Per Mare Per Terram* (1892), p. 146.

**Lan Kwai Fong**: Richard Sterling, Elizabeth Chong, and Lushan Charles Qin, *World Food Hong Kong (Lonely Planet World Food Guides)* (Footscray, Victoria: Lonely Planet Publications, 2001), p. 153.

**Lantau Island**: The Government of the Hong Kong Special Administrative Region, Lantau Development Task Force (2004), http://www.pland.gov.hk/pland_en/lantau/en/taskforce/index.html.

**Lantern Festival**: squarefoot.com.hk, "Living in Hong Kong: Chinese festivals" (2010), http://www.squarefoot.com.hk/section/chinese-festivals/.

**lap sap**: Brian Morton (ed.), *The Marine Flora and Fauna of Hong Kong and Southern China V: Proceedings of the Tenth International Marine Biological Workshop: The Marine Flora and Fauna of Hong Kong and Southern China, Hong Kong, 6026 April, 1998* (Hong Kong: Hong Kong University Press, 2000), p. 308.

**lap sap chung**: The Government of the Hong Kong Special Administrative Region, "Press release" (December 17, 2000), http://www.info.gov.hk/gia/general/200012/17/1216174.htm.

**lap-sap yan/lo/po**: ❶ Lex Lao, "Press enter." In Xu Xi and Mike Ingham (eds.), *City Voices: Hong Kong Writing in English, 1945 to the Present* (Hong Kong: Hong Kong University Press, 2003), p. 356. ❷ review33.com (2008), http://www.review33.com/palm/forum_msg_palm1.php?topic=78090319214736&number=254. ❸ Paps of Jura (2006), http://www.hkexpats.com/archive/index.php?t-5835.html.

**leng mo**: YesStyle.com, "PeopleStyle: Feature Ava Yu: On the way up" (2009), http://www.

yesstyle.com/en/peoplestyle-ava-yu-on-the-way-up/model.html/psid.40.

**leung**: Nicko Goncharoff and Damian Harper, *Hong Kong: City Guide* (Lonely Planet Publications, 1998), p. 58.

**li**: E. H. Parke, "A journey in north Sz Ch'uan" (continued from page 307). *The China Review, or Notes & Queries on the Far East*, 10(6) (1882), p. 365, http://sunzi1.lib.hku.hk/hkjo/view/26/2601263.pdf.

**li man fu**: Austin Coates, *Myself a Mandarin: Memoirs of a Special Magistrate* (Omaha, NE: The John Day Company, 1969), p. 13.

**linchi**: Clifford W. Collinson, *Half the Seas Over* (1933).

**ling chih**: F. S. Drake, "Nestorian crosses and Nestorian Christians in China under the Mongols." *Journal of the Hong Kong Branch of the Royal Asiatic Society*, 2 (1962): 11–25, 22.

**little brother**: Anonymous, "My story," Zi Teng Newsletter, Issue No. 14 (2004), http://www.ziteng.org.hk/newsletter/14_e.html#3.

**localization**: Savantas Policy Institute, "Policy and politics in Hong Kong" (2006), http://www.savantas.org/docs/HKU-PPAA-PolicyandPoliticsinHK.pdf.

**lolita**: ebay.com.hk, userid: littlegrocery, "Lolita & Fashion Accessories feature in Little Grocery" (1995–2010), http://cgi3.ebay.com.hk/ws/eBayISAPI.dll?ViewUserPage&userid=littlegrocery.

**lo mei**: The Government of the Hong Kong Special Administrative Region, Food and Environmental Hygiene Department, "Microbiological risk: Assessment of siu-mei and lo-mei in Hong Kong" (2001), *Risk Assessment Studies Report No. 6*, p. 5, http://www.cfs.gov.hk/english/programme/programme_haccp/files/report.pdf.

**lo mein**: Jiang Chenxin, "Waistlines key in health drive." *The Standard* (July 31, 2007), http://www.thestandard.com.hk/news_detail.asp?pp_cat=11&art_id=50208&sid=14713542&con_type=1.

**lucky money**: David Wallen, "Doctors' lucky money can buy good health in China." *The Standard* (May 13, 1996), http://www.thestandard.com.hk/archive_news_detail.asp?pp_cat=&art_id=38478&sid=&con_type=1&archive_d_str=19960513.

**Macanese**: ❶ China Travel Service (H.K.) Limited (2000–2010), www.ctshk.com/english/destination/macau/food.htm. ❷ Radio Television Hong Kong Online News, "Macanese go to polls today to choose legislators" (September 25, 2005), http://www.rthk.org.hk/rthk/news/englishnews/20050925/20050925_56_256930.html. ❸ Mike Chinoy, "Macanese population fears loss of identity." CNN.com, ASIANOW (December 18, 1999), http://archives.cnn.com/1999/ASIANOW/east/macau/stories/macau.macanese/.

**mafoo** (1): Ken Martinus, "Mafoos meeting to iron out problems." *The Standard* (May 3, 1996), http://www.thestandard.com.hk/archive_news_detail.asp?pp_cat=&art_id=61

649&sid=&con_type=1&archive_d_str=1996 0503.

**mafu**, also **mafoo** (2): ❶ The Government of the Hong Kong Special Administrative Region, in the High Court of the HKSAR Court of First Instance Magistracy, Appeal No. 818 of 2003 (on appeal from NKCC 3736/2003) (October 10, 2003). ❷ Keith Cho-kei Chau, "Policing prostitution in Hong Kong: An exploratory study in Mongkok District." M. Soc. Sc. thesis (Hong Kong: The University of Hong Kong, 2000), p. 42.

**mah-jong**, also **mahjongg**: ❶ Dr Wise on Risk Management (2006), http://www.sfc. hk/sfcPressRelease/EN/sfcOpenDocServ let?docno=06PR262. ❷ Chan Wing-Hoi, "Observations at the Jiu festival of Shek O and Tai Long Wan." *Journal of the Hong Kong Branch of the Royal Asiatic Society*, 26 (1986): 78–101, 79.

**mah-mah**: Emi, "Best of 3 worlds" (2009), http://triculturalbaby.blogspot.com/ 2009_03_01_archive.html.

**maid**: Santa Fe Relocation, "Domestic help" (n.d.), http://www.santaferelo.com/ecs/data/ sfguide/HKG/DomesticHelp.htm.

**mai dan**: Martin Booth, *Golden Boy: Memories of a Hong Kong Childhood* (New York: Thomas Dunne, 2005), p. 336.

**Mainland**: Yue-man Yeung (ed.), *The First Decade: The Hong Kong SAR in Retrospective and Introspective Perspectives* (Hong Kong: Chinese University Press, 2007), p. 203.

**Mainlander**: Eric Kit-wai Ma, *Culture, Politics, and Television in Hong Kong* (London: Routledge, 1999), p. 84.

**mamasan**: Timothy Mo, "Renegade or halo." In Xi Xu and Mike Ingham (ed.), *City Voices: Hong Kong Writing in English, 1945 to the Present* (Hong Kong: Hong Kong University Press, 2003), p. 91.

**mein**: "Mingling old with new." *The Hong Kong Standard* (April 19, 2006).

**Mid-Autumn Festival**: Jack C. Y. Cheng, Zarina C. L. Lam, P. C. Leung, and Diana Pansy Ma, "An epidemiological study on burn injuries in Hong Kong." *Journal of the Hong Kong Medical Association*, 42(1) (1990): 26–28, 27.

**Mid-Levels**: GoHome.com.hk, "Around Hong Kong: District Guide, Mid-Levels: West" (n.d.), http://www.gohome.com.hk/english/around_hk/info_one_district.asp?code=23.

**mil**: The Government of the Hong Kong Special Administrative Region, the Hong Kong Monetary Authority, Joseph Yam, chief executive, "Century-old treasures" (n.d.), http://www.info.gov.hk/hkma/eng/speeches/speechs/joseph/20040902e1.htm.

**ming pai**: Radha Chadha and Paul Husband, *The Cult of the Luxury Brand: Inside Asia's Love Affair with Luxury* (London; Boston: Nicholas Brealey International, 2006), pp. 167–169.

**Miss**: ytchan.com.hk, "Firm profile" (n.d.), http://www.ytchan.com.hk/pract_main.html.

**mm goi (saai)**: A Bluestocking Knits, "Hong Kong" (2005), http://mathomhouse.typepad.com/bluestocking/hong_kong/index.html.

**mm sai**: Nury Vittachi, edited by Stephanie Mitchell, *Goodbye Hong Kong, Hello Xianggang* (Hong Kong: O'Donald Publications, 1997), p. 74.

**mo lay tau**: Bob Hodge and Kam Louie, *The Politics of Chinese Language and Culture: The Art of Reading Dragons* (London: Routledge, 1998), p. 159.

**Monkey God Festival**: Jackie Sam, "Buddhist and Daoist devotees of Sun Wu-kong defy death: Monkey God's day inspires the bizarre." *The Standard* (September 20, 1996).

**moutai**: Ben Blanchard, "Mountain water packs punch." *The Standard* (February 9, 2007).

**mui tsai**: ❶ Irene Cheng, *Clara Ho Tung, A Hong Kong Lady: Her Family and Her Times* (Hong Kong: The Chinese University of Hong Kong, 1976), p. 177. ❷ "Girl enslaved, beaten by aunt in rare case." *The Standard* (December 9, 2006).

**mushroom pavilion/hut**: ❶ The Government of the Hong Kong Special Administrative Region, Education Bureau (n.d.), cd1.edb.hkedcity. net/cd/wcms/6371/Tourism%20English.ppt. ❷ June Ng, "Hut hunting." HK-magazine. com (June 8, 2010), http://hk.asia-city.com/restaurants/article/hut-hunting.

**National Day**: Joseph Y. S Cheng (eds.), *The Other Hong Kong Report, 1997* (Hong Kong: Chinese University Press, 1997), p. 521.

**New Kowloon**: S. F. Richards, "Contemporary features of the population of Hong Kong." In R. D. Hill and Jennifer Bray (eds.), *Geography and the Environment in*

*Southeast Asia* (Hong Kong: Hong Kong University Press, 1978), p. 370.

**New Territories**: benchjade, "My Hongkong Tour" (2008), http://www.skyscrapercity.com/showthread.php?t=625782.

**ni hao**: Wendy (2008), Forum@Isaacspace.hk, http://www.isaacspace.hk/forum/archiver/?tid-14.html.

**Noonday Gun**: The Government of the Hong Kong Special Administrative Region, Home Affairs Department, "Welcome to 'Hong Kong Fun in 18 Districts'" (2005), http://www.gohk.gov.hk/text/eng/welcome/east_route.html.

**nullah**: The Government of the Hong Kong Special Administrative Region, Development Bureau, "16 nullahs will be decked in 10 years" (January 14, 2005), http://sc.info.gov.hk/gb/www. news.gov.hk/en/category/environment/050114/html/050114en04007.htm.

**OK**: The Government of the Hong Kong Special Administrative Region, Karaoke Establishments Ordinance, Section 2, Subsection 1 (2002).

**Old China Hand**: Mark Roberti, *The Fall of Hong Kong: China's Triumph and Britain's Betrayal* (New York: John Wiley and Sons, 1994), p. 37.

**one big pot wages**: Chris Rowley and Robert Fitzgerald, "Hong Kong's development: Prospects and possibilities." In Chris Rowley and Robert Fitzgerald (eds.), *Managed in Hong Kong: Adaptive Systems Entrepreneurship and Human Resources* (London: Frank Cass, 2000), p. 129.

**one country two systems**: Joseph Yam, "Monetary arrangements under 'One Country, Two Systems'" (updated September 20, 1997), http://www.info.gov.hk/hkma/eng/speeches/speechs/joseph/speech_200997b.htm.

**overtime**: Richard Welford and Shalini Mahtani, "Work life balance in Hong Kong: Survey results" (2004), http://british.e-consulate.org/csr/Work%20Life%20Balance.pdf, p. 2.

**paddy**: Harold Ingrams, *Hong Kong* (London: Her Majesty's Stationery Office, 1952), p. 178.

**pai lau**: The Government of the Hong Kong Special Administrative Region, Civil Engineering and Development Department, "Newsletter, 27" (2009), p. 5, http://www.cedd.gov.hk/eng/publications/newsletter/doc/cedd_newsletter_27.pdf.

**pajamas**, also **pyjamas**: ❶ Frank Viviano, "City of the main chance." In James O'Reilly, Larry Habegger, and Sean O'Reilly (eds.), *Travelers' Tales Hong Kong: True Stories of Life on the Road* (San Francisco: Travelers' Tales, Inc., 1996), p. 19. ❷ The 19th International Conference on Pattern Recognition, Hong Kong (September 3–7, 2006), p. 7, www.comp.hkbu.edu.hk/~yytang/ICPR06-to-U.pdf.

**pak pai**: Hong Kong Legislative Council, "Official report of proceedings," Wednesday, December 3, 1969, http://www.legco.gov.hk/yr69-70/h691203.pdf.

**palm civet**: Chun Yip Lam, "Comparative molecular analysis of the binding between severe acute respiratory syndrome coronavirus (SARS-CoV) spike protein and angiotensin converting enzyme 2 (ACE2)." M.Phil. thesis (Hong Kong: The University of Hong Kong, 2007), abstract.

**panel teacher**: Inland Revenue Board of Review Decisions, Case No. D62197 (n.d.), p. 5, http://www.info.gov.hk/bor/eng/pdf/dv12_second/d6297.pdf.

**pang uk**: Bernie Owen and Raynor Shaw, *Hong Kong Landscapes: Shaping the Barren Rock* (Hong Kong: Hong Kong University Press, 2007), p. 151.

**pantyhose tea/coffee**: ❶ Sylvia Hui, "'Pantyhose tea' has leg up in Hong Kong." Associated Press (Monday, March 6, 2006). ❷ AboutHK, "Hong Kong-style milk tea" (August 11, 2007), http://www.abouthk.com/index.php?option=com_content&view=article&id=13:hong-kong-style-milk-tea&catid=27:food&Itemid=47.

**Parsi**, also **Parsee**: ❶ The Central School, Hong Kong (n.d.), www.lcsd.gov.hk/CE/Museum/Monument/form/AAB123_Annex_A.pdf. ❷ Plaque in the Main Building of the University of Hong Kong.

**passport holder**: Tsang Yok Sing, "Fuel to the ire?" *South China Morning Post* (June 3, 2008).

**passport prison**: Carine Lai, "The values of July 1" (Part 2). Civic Express, Hong Kong's Blogazine (April 10, 2006), http://www.civic-express.com/carine/?p=37.

**passport widow**: Larry Feign, *Postcards from Lily Wong* (Hong Kong: Macmillan Publishers Ltd., 1990), p. 90.

**Pearl of the Orient/East:** ❶ N. Mark Lam and John L. Graham, *China Now: Doing Business in the World's Most Dynamic Market* (New York: McGraw-Hill, 2006), p. 237. ❷ Siu-kai Lau (ed.), *The First Tung Chee-hwa Administration: The First Five Years of the Hong Kong Special Administration Region* (Hong Kong: Chinese University Press, 2002), p. 2.

**penang lawyer:** Herbert Giles, "Short notices of new books." *The China Review, or Notes & Queries on the Far East*, 6(5) (1878): 331–339, 333.

**picul:** G. B. Endacott and Alan Birch, *Hong Kong Eclipse* (Hong Kong: Oxford University Press, 1978), p. 21.

**poon choi:** Leslie Kwoh, "New Year gets off to sickly start." *The Standard* (February 2, 2006).

**po-po**, also **pohpo, pohpoh:** ❶ Larry Feign, *Banned in Hong Kong* (Hong Kong: Hambalan, 1995), p. 126. ❷ Xu Xi, *The Unwalled City* (Hong Kong: Chameleon Press, 2001), p. 161. ❸ The Hoobastank Message Boards, powered by MyLocalBands.com, userid: The Pilar (January 8, 2007), http://post.mylocalbands. com/post.asp?xid=6&forum=0&topic=13464 95&page=2&sk=.

**pork chop:** Margaret Wu, Lingnan University, Equal Opportunities Commission, "Sexual Harassment on Campus" (2008), www.ln.edu. hk/poccb/activities/sh_eoc.ppt, slide 14.

**praya:** Urban Council, *City of Victoria* (Hong Kong: Urban Council, 1994), p. 42.

**princeling:** Matthew Fletcher and Law Siu Lan, "Burning bright: China Everbright is Hong

Kong's hottest company. Can it deliver?" *Asiaweek* (1997), http://www.asiaweek.com/asiaweek/97/0627/biz1.html.

**pro-China**: Ming K. Chan (ed.), *The Challenge of Hong Kong's Reintegration with China* (Hong Kong: Hong Kong University Press, 1997), p. 135.

**Pu-er**: Mobius International Limited, "Product catalogue (2000–2010)," http://www.mobius.com.hk/products.htm.

**Punti**: ❶ Nicole Constable, *Christian Souls and Chinese Spirits: A Hakka Community in Hong Kong* (Berkeley: University of California Press, 1994), p. 188. ❷ Nicole Constable (ed.), *Guest People: Hakka Identity in China and Abroad* (Seattle: University of Washington Press, 2005), p. 10.

**Putonghua**: Wei-Bin Zhang, *Hong Kong: The Pearl Made of British Mastery and Chinese Docile-Diligence* (New York: Nova Science Publishers, 2006), p. 123.

**qigong**: Emily Ashman, "Staycations." *HK Magazine* (August 4, 2006).

**red capitalist**: Rafferty Kevin, *City on the Rocks: Hong Kong's Uncertain Future* (London: Viking, 1990), p. 335.

**red chip**: Fulton Mak, "Red chips eye A-share options." *The Standard* (May 18, 2007), http://www.thestandard.com.hk/news_detail.asp?we_cat=2&art_id=44732&sid=13663365&con_type=1&d_str=20070518&fc=8.

**red packet/pocket money**: ❶ The Government of the Hong Kong Special Administrative Region. Education Bureau, "Enhancing thinking skills in science context: Teachers' reference. Lesson 1, *Nature of Science*" (n.d.), http://resources.edb.gov.hk/gifted/tr/thinking_skills/, p. 2. ❷ Janny's Cooking Diary, "Red pocket money" (February 5, 2008), http://jannyscookingdiary.blogspot.com/2008/02/red-pocket-money.html.

**red pole (fighter)**: *South China Morning Post* (September 11, 2009), C1.

**Renminbi**: Dror Poleg, "China currency: Trade, revaluation, exchange rate." Danwei (April 9, 2005), www.danwei.org/china_information/china_currency_trade_revaluati.php.

**reprovisioning**: The Government of the Hong Kong Special Administrative Region, Environment, Transport and Works Bureau, "Press release: Reprovisioning Sha Tin water treatment works" (2004), http://www.etwb.gov.hk/press_releases_and_publications/press_releases/index.aspx?langno=1&nodeid=778&Branch=W&lstYear=2004&PressReleaseID=8477.

**rice Christian**: Andrew Williamson, *The Chinese Business Puzzle: How to Work More Effectively with Chinese Cultures* (Oxford: How To Books, 2003), p. 81.

**rickshaw**: The Government of the Hong Kong Special Administrative Region, "The laws of Hong Kong: Road traffic (Registration and licensing of vehicles) regulations," Chapter 374E, Regulation 40, licensing of rickshaws, part VII (June 30, 1997), http://www.legislation.gov.hk/blis_ind.nsf/CurAllEngDoc/ 5FF6E24ACDD0C246C8256483002AAC7E?OpenDocument.

**right of abode**: Hong Kong Human Rights Monitor, "New survey on right of abode casts doubt on government's 'taxi method' survey" (October 18, 1999), http://www.hkhrm.org.hk/english/reports/press/pr181099.html.

**rubbish**: The Government of the Hong Kong Special Administrative Region, "Press release: Clean Hong Kong Day" (1999), http://www.info.gov.hk/gia/general/199912/05/1205120.htm.

**salt-baked chicken**: "Hakka Ye Ye." *HK Magazine*, http://hk-magazine.com/review/hakka-ye-ye.

**samfoo**, also **samfu**: ❶ Jason Wordie, *Streets: Exploring Hong Kong Island* (Hong Kong: Hong Kong University Press, 2002), p. 109. ❷ Don Quixote in China (n.d.), www.deanbarrettmystery.com/don_quixote_in_china2.htm.

**sampan**: The Government of the Hong Kong Special Administrative Region, Marine Department, "Sinking of sampan resulting in fatality at Tai Long Wan" (April 29, 2004), www.mardep.gov.hk/en/publication/pdf/mai040429.pdf.

**sampan congee**: Bupa Health Insurance, "Health gallery: Health tips" (2008), http://www.bupa.com.hk/en/healthgallery/healthtips/show.aspx?c=2&id=10154.

**samshu**, also **samsu**, **samshoo**: ❶ Chan Man-fai, "The development of the forensic services in Hong Kong." M. Soc. Sc. thesis (Hong Kong: The University of Hong Kong, 1992), p. 30. ❷ Lennox A. Mills, *British Rule in Eastern Asia: A Study of Contemporary Government* *and Economic Development in British Malaya and Hong Kong* (London: Oxford University Press, 1942), p. 232. ❸ F. Hirth, "The Peninsula of Lei-chow (concluded)." *The China Review* 2(6) (1874): 341–351, 348.

**sandwich class**: Richard Wong, "The budget, inflation, and housing." *The Hong Kong Centre For Economic Research* (originally published 1992), http://www.hku.hk/hkcer/articles/v14/rwong.htm.

**sars**: Christian Stauffer, "Market view." *Trade and Forfaiting Review* 7(6) (2004): 5.

**school brother/sister**: ❶ *The Prisoner*. DVD Movie Central (n.d.), http://www.dvdmoviecentral.com/ReviewsText/prisoner_jackie_chan.htm. ❷ Groovy Pinky Diary, "Diary" (August 19, 2007), http://modernzarn14.blogspot.com/search/label/diary.

**second kitchen**: ❶ Robin Hutcheon, *China-Yellow* (Hong Kong: Chinese University Press, 1996), p. 421. ❷ Kathleen Cheek-Milby, *A Legislature Comes of Age: Hong Kong's Search for Influence and Identity*, vol. 2 (Hong Kong: Oxford University Press, 1995), p. 283.

**sedan chair**: ❶ Hugh D. R. Baker, *Hong Kong Images: People and Animals* (Hong Kong: Hong Kong University Press, 1990), p. 22. ❷ Jason Y. Ng, "The dark history of sedan chairs" (November 17, 2008), http://jasonyng.blogspot.com/2008_11_01_archive.html.

**Sevens, Hong Kong**: May Holdsworth (with additional text by Caroline Courtauld): *Foreign Devils: Expatriates in Hong Kong* (Oxford: Oxford University Press, 2002), p. 260.

**Seven Sisters Festival**: Janice E. Stockard, *Daughters of the Canton Delta: Marriage Patterns and Economic Strategies in South China, 1860–1930* (Hong Kong: Hong Kong University Press, 1992), p. 43.

**shan**: Michael Ingham, *Hong Kong: A Cultural History* (New York: Oxford University Press, 2007), p. 107.

**Shanghai foot**: Hannelore Heinemann Headly, *Blond China Doll: A Shanghai Interlude, 1939–1953* (St. Catharines, Ont.: Blond China Doll Enterprises, 2004), p. 87.

**Shanghailanders**: Felix Patrikeeff, *Mouldering Pearl: Hong Kong at the Crossroads* (London: George Philip, 1989), p. 56.

**Shanghainese**: Siu-lun Wong, "The migration of Shanghainese entrepreneurs to Hong Kong." In David Faure, James Hayes, and Alan Birch (eds.), *From Village to City: Studies in the Traditional Roots of Hong Kong Society* (Hong Kong: Centre of Asian Studies, the University of Hong Kong, 1984), p. 206.

**shoe of gold**: K. Stevens, "Altar images from Hunan and Kiangsi." *Journal of the Hong Kong Branch of the Royal Asiatic Society*, 18 (1978): 41–48, 46.

**shoeshine boy**, also **shoe-shiner**: ❶ Review33 (n.d.), http://m.review33.com/forum_msg.php?db=3&topic=26090821214556&start=100&sort=1. ❷ Hemlock's diary (August 2006), http://www.geocities.com/hkhemlock/dog/diary-19aug06.html.

**short-time hotel**: William Sparrow, "The lady works alone—or does she?" Asian Sex

Gazette: China Sex (November 9, 2005), http://www.asiansexgazette.com/asg/china/china05news21.htm.

**shroff**: The Government of the Hong Kong Special Administrative Region, Hong Kong Housing Authority, "Rent payment methods" (2009), http://www.housingauthority.gov.hk/en/residential/guidestools/rentpayment/.

**shroffing**: The Government of the Hong Kong Special Administrative Region, Government Logistics Department, "Advertising in the Government of the HKSAR Gazette" (2004), http://www.gld.gov.hk/eng/services_6.htm.

**-side**: The Chinese University of Hong Kong, Information Technology in English Language Teaching Conference website, "About Hong Kong" (2006), http://www.cuhk.edu.hk/eltu/tcelt/conference/2006/abouthkp.htm.

**sifu**: Hazel Clark, *The Cheongsam* (Oxford: Oxford University Press, 2000), p. 32.

**silk-stocking milk tea**: Christopher DeWolf, "Morning coffee: The boss" (April 9, 2007), http://www.urbanphoto.net/blog/2007/04/09/morning-coffee-8-the-boss/.

**sitting-out area**: Ginger Thrash, *Above The City: Hiking Hong Kong Island* (Hong Kong: Hong Kong University Press, 2005), p. 59.

**siu mai**, also **shu mai**, **shao mai**: ❶ Lingnan University, "A student project by Ho Sin Ting, Sandy Ho Wing Yan, Wing; Instructor: Dr. Ziyou Yu" (n.d.), http://www.library.ln.edu.hk/lingnan/studproj/business/docs/bba03_01.pdf. ❷ DarkLegion Forums, "Jet Li: What's making you HAPPY today?"

(October 1, 2009), http://karenmok.com/bbs/thread-13815-38-1.html. ❸ Muhammad Cohen, *Hong Kong on Air* (Hong Kong: Blacksmith Books, 2007), p. 24.

**siu mei**: docstoc.com. "A guide to application for siu mei and lo mei shop license" (n.d.). http://www.docstoc.com/docs/3415938/A-GUIDE-TO-APPLICATION-FOR-SIU-MEI-AND-LO-MEI.

**small chow**: Robert S. Elegant, *Last Year in Hong Kong: A Love Story* (New York: William Morrow and Company, 1997), p. 114.

**smelly (stinky) tofu**: "Hong Kong eats: Street eats and treats." *South China Morning Post* (March 6, 2008), http://www.scmp.com.hk/portal/site/SCMP/menuitem.c218a8e69dce44a38ce4cb10cba0a0a0/ ?cat=Hong%20Kong%20Eats&ss=archives&s=video&pgIdx=2.

**snakehead**: ❶ Hong Kong Human Rights Commission Society for Community Organization, "Urgent appeal to the United Nations Committee on the Rights of the Child" (n.d.), http://www.lasalle.org.hk/rightsofchild/viii3.doc. ❷ John Burnett, *Dangerous Waters: Modern Piracy and Terror on the High Seas* (New York: Dutton Adult, 2002), p. 219.

**SoHo**: HKGOLD, "Music appreciation" (n.d.), http://gold2.ieee.org.hk/wiki/index.php/Music_Appreciation.

**spiders**, also **spidermen**: ❶ Hong Kong, Asia's World City, "Buildings and bridges" (n.d.), http://mobile.brandhk.gov.hk/en/myHK/building.php. ❷ CityLife, "A Hong Kong travel guide" (2008), http://www.citylifehk.com/citylife/eng/cover_1107.jsp.

**spirit money**, also **paper money**, **hell money**, **hell bank notes**: ❶ Moh Keed Wong, Kwai Pik Wan, and Fung Fong Siew (eds.), *To My Heart, with Smiles: The Love Letters of Siew Fung Fong & Wan Kwai Pik, 1920–1941* (Singapore: Landmark Books, 1988), p. 57. ❷ B. D. Wilson, "Chinese burial customs in Hong Kong." *Journal of the Hong Kong Branch of the Royal Asiatic Society*, 1 (1961): 115–123, 119. ❸ Cat Yronwode, "Hell money (hell bank notes)." Luckymojo (1995), http://www.luckymojo.com/hellmoney.html.

**splittist**: The Hong Kong Journalists Association (HKJA), "Submission to the United Nations Human Rights Committee on the Hong Kong Special Administrative Region's implementation of the International Covenant on Civil and Political Rights" (September 6, 1999), http://www.legco.gov.hk/yr98-99/english/panels/ha/papers/ha23091a.htm.

**staffs**: Yin Cheong Cheng, *New Paradigm for Re-engineering Education: Globalization, Localization and Individualization* (Dordrecht: Springer, 2005), p. 200.

**Suzie Wong**: Transforming Asian Education: Through Open and Distance Learning website, the Open University of Hong Kong, "Hong Kong City Tour" (n.d.), http://www.ouhk.edu.hk/cridal/cridala2005/hong_kong_city_tour.html.

**swallow nest**: The City University of Hong Kong, CTL5403 Semantics and Discourse,

Assignment One. The first course at the dinner was Chinese swallow-nest soup (March 9, 2006), http://ctlhpan.cityu.edu.hk/haihuapan/course/ctl5403/ctl5403-Assignment1.doc.

**sycee**: Betty Peh-T'i Wei, *Ruan Yuan, 1764–1849: The Life and Work of a Major Scholar-Official in Nineteenth-Century China before the Opium War* (Hong Kong: Hong Kong University Press, 2006), p. 135.

**tael**: Hong Kong Consumer Council (1997), http://www.consumer.org.hk/website/ws_en/news/press_releases/p243.html.

**taikonaut**: The Government of the Hong Kong Special Administrative Region, Leisure and Cultural Services Department, "Press release: Exhibition on China's first manned space mission' starts today" (November 1, 2003).

**taipan**: Urban Council, *City of Victoria* (Hong Kong: Urban Council, 1994), p. 15.

**tai-tai**: Nury Vittachi, *The Hong Kong Joke Book* (Hong Kong: Chameleon Press, 1995), p. 72.

**tai-tai lunch**: Susanna Hoe, *The Private Life of Old Hong Kong: Western Women in the British Colony 1841–1941* (Hong Kong: Oxford University Press, 1991), p. 13.

**Tam Kung Festival**: Yiu Kong Chu, *The Triads as Business* (London: Routledge, 2000), p. 37.

**tang yuan**, also **tong yuen**: ❶ Vocational Training Council, Tsing Yi Language Centre, "Language Connect 3" (2010), p. 2. ❷ Wellcome, "Wellcome reminisces Chinese customs with customers exclusive promotions and

Chinese New Year merchandise on offer" (January 18, 2010), http://www.wellcome. com.hk/en/files/data/89ae9125db52568 d1cddf281f2f9f06e.pdf.

**tea money**: Jung-Fang Tsai, *Hong Kong in Chinese History: Community and Social Unrest in the British Colony, 1842–1913* (New York: Columbia University Press, 1995), p. 109.

**ten thousand steps**: "Tseung Kwan O: Health City, Project Office" (n.d.), http://www.cse.ust. hk/~anlu/Photos/Walk10K/index.html.

**three-legged stool**: The Knowledge Management Branch of DPADM/UNDESA, "Governance world watch 100" (2007). http://www. unpan.org/directory/worldNews/include/ displayIssueDetail.asp?issueID=35.

**tiffin**: The Open University of Hong Kong, "A history of Hong Kong 1842–1984" (n.d.), http://www.ouhk.edu.hk/~etpwww/oustyle/ aw213.pdf.

**tin fong wife**: Hong Kong, District Court, The Hong Kong Law Reports (1962), p. 677.

**Tin Hau**: Marimari.com, "Hong Kong—Kowloon" (n.d.), http://www.marimari.com/cOnTENT/ hong_kong/popular_places/kowloon/main. html.

**Tin Hau Festival**: James Hayes, *Tsuen Wan: Growth of a 'New Town' and Its People* (Hong Kong: Oxford University Press, 1993), p. 152.

**tin kau**: J. S. Lam, "Cops win as stations lose gamble." *The Standard* (August 30, 2010), http://www.thestandard.com.hk/news_print. asp?art_id=102266&sid=29338011.

**tofu**: William Pesek, "Tofu buildings raise inflation risks." *The Standard* (May 27, 2008), http://www.thestandard.com.hk/news_detail.asp?pp_cat=15&art_id=66363&sid=19085987&con_type=1.

**tong** (1): Bertil Lintner, *Blood Brothers: Crime, Business and Politics in Asia* (Crows Nest, NSW: Allen and Unwin, 2002), p. 119.

**tong** (2): ❶ Shu-min Huang, "Impacts of British colonial administration on Hong Kong's land tenure system." *New Asia Academic Bulletin*, 6 (1986): 10. ❷ The Law Reform Commission, "Law changes recommended on inheritance," p. 5.

**tong fai**: St. Louis School Circular No. 98 (September 2008).

**tong gau**: STOP, "Save HK's cats and dogs: Why we need STOP" (2009), http://www.hkstop.org/en/needSTOP.php.

**tong lau**: Katty Law of the Central and Western Concern Group, quoted in an article by Sarah Fung, "Love Your Tong Lau," in *HK Magazine* (September 2009).

**tong sui**: Richard Sterling, Elizabeth Chong, and Lushan Charles Qin, *World Food Hong Kong (Lonely Planet World Food Guides)* (Footscray, Victoria: Lonely Planet Publications, 2001), p. 119.

**triad**: ❶ The Open University of Hong Kong, "From triad member to role model." Openlink, 15(4) (2010), http://www.ouhk.edu.hk/WCM/ ?FUELAP_TEMPLATENAME=tcGenericPage&itemid=CC_OPENLINK_57624598&lang=eng. ❷ W. P. Morgan, *Triad Societies*

*in Hong Kong* (Hong Kong: Government
Printer, 1960), p. 3.

**tso:** ❶ The District Court of the Hong Kong
Special Administrative Region, Civil Action
No. 661 of 2007. Between the Plaintiff, Sum
Koon Tai, Shum Tin Yeung and Sum Wong
On as the managers of Sham Kiu Ming Tso,
and the Defendant, Au Cheung (2007).
❷ Shu-Ming Huang, "Impacts of British
colonial administration on Hong Kong's
land tenure system." *New Asia Academic
Bulletin* 6 (1986): 3–21, 3.

**Tuen Ng**: Michael Ingham, *Hong Kong: A Cultural
History* (New York: Oxford University Press,
2007), p. 142.

**turnip**: Lee Kum Kee homepage (2003), http://
hk.lkk.com/kitchen/recipe_details.asp?choic
e=1&veg=0&sauceid=64&Page=3&isCat=0&r
ecipeid=944.

**turnip cake**: HKedCity, "English Campus" (2003),
http://www.hkedcity.net/english/create/
view_file1.phtml?file_id=25485.

**turtle's egg**, also **turtle egg**: ❶ Ailing Zhang, *Naked
Earth: A Novel about China* (Hong Kong:
Union Press, 1964), p. 100. ❷ UO—Ultima
Online, "Guild War: SM vs X78" (2009),
www.playuo.net/archiver/?tid-3415.html.

**typhoon signal number**: Career Times Online
Limited, "Typhoon attack and compulsory
work on rest days" (2009), http://
careertimes.com.hk/english/article/
show_article.asp?filename=BLPHD_0209200
204.asp&type=LP&subtype=HD&page=1&bro
wser=netscape.

**uncle**: Mandatory Provident Fund Schemes Authority, "Differences between an MPF scheme and an ORSO scheme" (2008), http://www.mpfa.org.hk/english/quicklinks/quicklinks_pub/files/ORSO_leaflet_Eng.pdf.

**unlucky draw**: Patsy Moy and Alex Lo, "Nurse feels cheated by unlucky draw for Sars ward." *South China Morning Post* (April 19, 2003), p. C1.

**vocabularies**: Synergy Technologies (Asia) Limited, "Press release: The lightest PDA phone GIGABYTE g-Smart is officially launched in Hong Kong and Macau" (June 1, 2006), http://www.synergy-asia.com.hk/rc2/event/press_release_060601.asp.

**waah**, also **wah**: ❶ Karen (2005), http://allolalia.idenise.net/karen/?m=200503&paged=2. ❷ Larry Feign, *Banned in Hong Kong* (Hong Kong: Hambalan, 1995), p. 68.

**wai**: J. S. Lam, "Bloody terror on 'The Gap' night patrol." *The Standard* (July 8, 2010), p. 14, http://www.thestandard.com.hk/news_detail.asp?we_cat=5&art_id=100221&sid=28750457&con_type=1&d_str=20100708&fc=2.

**wallah wallah**, also **walla-walla**: ❶ The Government of the Hong Kong Special Administrative Region, Environmental Protection Department, "Central reclamation, phase III, studies, site investigation, design and construction: Environmental impact assessment report 1" (2001), 1.5.1. ❷ The 1998 Hong Kong Diving Guide (1998), http://www.scuba.net.hk/oceanway/Local%20dive/ds_gruff.htm.

**wan yee**: Joyce Kam, "Hearty fare for holidays." *The Standard* (January 13, 2009), http://www.thestandard.com.hk/news_detail.asp?we_cat=16&art_id=76907&sid=22216022&con_type=3&d_str=20090113&fc=3.

**wet market**: Terri Mottershead, *Sustainable Development in Hong Kong* (Hong Kong: Hong Kong University Press, 2004), p. 508.

**white elephant**: Nury Vittachi, *The Shanghai Union of Industrial Mystics* (Edinburgh: Polygon, 2007), p. 291.

**white gold**: The Government of the Hong Kong Special Administrative Region, "Legislative Council Panel on Economic Development proposed amendments to the trade descriptions ordinance and its subsidiary legislation to strengthen consumer protection" (October 22, 2007), CB(1)76/07-08(02).

**white tiger**: mypleasureforum.com, "Bonnie's gals past & present" (2009), www.mypleasureforum.com/showthread.php? p=7196.

**winter congos**: Alain Le Pichon, *China Trade and Empire: Jardine, Matheson & Co. and the Origins of British Rule in Hong Kong, 1827–1843* (New York: Oxford University Press, 2006), p. 213.

**Wishing Tree**: Michael Ingham, *Hong Kong: A Cultural History* ( New York: Oxford University Press, 2007), p. 222.

**wok**: ❶ Robert Fell, "Towards the Unified Exchange" (1992), p. 17, http://www.sfc.hk/sfc/doc/EN/speeches/public/others/speechbook/chapter1.pdf. ❷ Dan Waters,"Laughter across The Great

Wall: A comparison of Chinese and Western humour." *Journal of the Hong Kong Branch of the Royal Asiatic Society* 38 (1998): 1–50, 17.

**wonton**: she.com (2004), http://community.she.com/messageboard/career/?action=view.topic&id=799990&ref=msg.cat.lp.

**wushu**: Mark Jancovich, *Defining Cult Movies: The Cultural Politics of Oppositional Taste* (Manchester: Manchester University Press, 2003), p. 169.

**xiao long bao**: Computer World Hong Kong, "Made to order" (n.d.), http://www.cw.com.hk/computerworldhk/article/articleDetail.jsp?id=375949.

**XO sauce**: Lee Kum Kee, "Lee Kum Kee products" (n.d.), http://hk.lkk.com/product/product_details.asp?cat=6.

**ya-ya**: Sarah Woods, *Adventures with Kids: The Essential Guide to Hong Kong for the Expat Parent* (Hong Kong: Handy Guides, 2004), p. 41.

**yellow fever**: Hongkie Town, userid: Spike (March 3, 2007), http://laowai.blogspot.com/.

**yeuk**: Urban Council, *City of Victoria* (Hong Kong: Urban Council, 1994), p. 1.

**ye ye**: Adeline Yen Mah, *Chinese Cinderella: The True Story of an Unwanted Daughter* (New York: Laurel-Leaf, 2001), p. 17.

**yin-yang**, also **yuen yen**, **yuan yang**: ❶ Sylvia Hui, "'Pantyhose tea' has leg up in Hong Kong." Associated Press (Monday, March 6, 2006). ❷ Richard Sterling, Elizabeth Chong, and Lushan Charles Qin, *World Food Hong Kong (Lonely Planet World Food*

*Guides)* (Footscray, Victoria: Lonely Planet Publications, 2001), p. 173. ❸ Tsit Wing Coffee Co. Limited Food wrapper.

**yuan**: City University Hong Kong (n.d.), http://www.ee.cityu.edu.hk/~agec/travel.htm.

**Yue Lan**: Janet W. Salaff, *Working Daughters of Hong Kong: Filial Piety or Power in the Family?* (Cambridge: Cambridge University Press, 1981), p. 181.

**yuen**: Martin Williams, Hong Kong Outdoors, "Lung Tsai Ng Yuen: A Chinese landscaped garden on Lantau Island, HK" (2004), http://www.hkoutdoors.com/lantau-island/ng-yuen-lantau.html.

**yum cha**: ❶ Betty Wei and Elizabeth Li, *Culture Shock! Hong Kong: A Survival Guide to Customs and Etiquette*, second edition (Singapore, Times Books International, 1998), p. 171. ❷ AboutHK.com, "More information about HK" (n.d.), http://www.abouthk.com/news/newslist.php?typeid=163&sType=167.

**yum cha house**: Richard Sterling, Elizabeth Chong, and Lushan Charles Qin, *World Food Hong Kong (Lonely Planet World Food Guides)* (Footscray, Victoria: Lonely Planet Publications, 2001), p. 173.

**yum sing**, also **yum seng**: ❶ Marya Glyn-Daniel, *Hong Kong Lover* (Victoria, BC: Trafford Publishing, 2007), p. 180. ❷ Music Videos, utac (2010), www.musicvideo.idv.hk/tag_utac.html.

**yum-yum girl**: Tom Carter, Travel and Leisure, "Down and out in Hong Kong" (May 28,

2007), http://leisureandtravels.blogspot.
com/2007/05/down-out-in-hong-kong.html.